THE BOMBING

The following people gave me information concerning the raids on Bath. In the case of some married women, the names given are those they hold today:

Bernard Astley-Weston, Casualty officer
Herbert Bath, Fireman
William Burden, Firewatcher
Jill Clayton, Schoolgirl
Emily Coleman, WVS
Sidney Coleman, Warden
Eric Davies, Soldier
Albert Davies, Rescue worker
Florence Delve
William Delve, Factory worker
Faith Dolman, Schoolgirl
Ken Drew, Messenger
Rosalind Field
Tom Gale, Fireman
Edith Gingell
Henry Gough, Soldier
Muriel Gough
Henry Hamlin, Rescue worker
Elizabeth Harden
William Harris, Despatch rider
Sam Hayward, Firewatcher
Ivy Hemingway
Majorie Horsell, First aider
Bernard Humphries
Edward Hurford
Winifred Hurford
Mr. Jackson, Police
Hubert Jackson, Admiralty
Frederick Kohn, Hospital Supervisor
Betty Lee

Geoffrey Lock, Chief warden
Anne Marks, Schoolgirl
Ethel Martin
Myrtle Meredith, Office worker
Rose Miller
Kathleen Muse, Schoolgirl
Leslie Nott, Despatch rider
Mary Nott, CD worker
Vic Penny, Ambulance driver
Reg Polden, Warden
Mrs. Potter, Schoolgirl
Anthony Self, Schoolboy
Frank Selwyn, Firewatcher
Grace Selwyn, First aider
Ron Shearn, Warden
Fred Short, Rescue worker
Doris Smith, Ambulance driver
Doris Smith
Dorothy Smith, Schoolgirl
Robert Smith, Ambulance driver
William Smith, Ambulance driver
Edwin Stainer, Schoolboy
Kathleen Stainer, Schoolgirl
Walter Sweetenham, Schoolboy
Don Tuddenham, First aider
Betty Tutt, Schoolgirl
Doreen Wall, Secretary
Mary Warne, Schoolgirl
James Webster, Firewatcher
Mark Whiteley, Schoolboy

THE BOMBING OF BATH

by

NIALL ROTHNIE

*The German Air Raids of
April 1942*

DEDICATION

In memory of my father, Andrew Rothnie

FOLLY BOOKS

Second Edition Folly Books 2010

First published by Ashgrove Press Ltd, 1983

A catalogue record for this book is available from the
British Library

ISBN 978-0-9564405-1-8

Published by Folly Books
Monkton Farleigh
BA15 2QP
www.follybooks.co.uk

Typeset by Vicky

Printed and bound in Great Britain by
J F Print Ltd, Sparkford

Editor's Introduction

Shortly after the first edition of this book was published in 1983 the Royal Photographic Society put on an exhibition of contemporary photographs entitled *Bath Blitz* at the Octagon in Bath's Milsom Street which, for a relatively short period, housed the headquarters of the society. At much the same time I was involved with the restoration of Monkton Farleigh Mine and setting it up as a museum. The mine, beneath a hillside some four miles east of Bath, above the village of Bathford, was a former underground Bath stone quarry that had been converted by the War Office during the late 1930s into the largest underground ammunition storage depot in the world. This work was part of a vast and secret programme of military construction undertaken in preparation for the Second World War, which the strategists of the time knew was inevitable. The surface reception area in which our customers waited before being taken underground on guided tours contained a range of displays on various military or home-front themes. After the *Bath Blitz* exhibition at the Royal Photographic Society came to the end of its rather short run we successfully negotiated with the society to acquire all the images (100 or so large, mounted photographs) for exhibition at the mine. Subsequently these images, together with a few others acquired from private collections and a larger number of specially commissioned contemporary photographs of Bath's wartime bomb-sites taken for comparison purposes, provided the core of a permanent *Bombing of Bath* interpretive display that ran for more than six years.

The exhibition was well received by our visitors but the almost universal response, not just from tourists from distant parts of Britain and around the world but also from local residents was most extraordinary:

'I didn't know that Bath was bombed!'

It was as if an encapsulated era of the City's past – the whole of the wartime years – had been expunged from recorded history, apart, perhaps, from the fact that rather a large number of Civil Servants, employees of the Admiralty, had been evacuated to Bath in 1939 and subsequently seemed markedly reluctant to leave at the war's end. There are many reasons for this apparent historical amnesia. After five years of conflict everyone was heartily sick of war; there was a deep desire to forget the past and start life anew. Despite the austerity of the late 1940s and of the following dreary decade, Britain was bathed in the quiet confidence of a bright new future in which the whole population, from pauper to peer – supported cradle-to-grave by the new Welfare State – would never have had it so good. By the end of the war residents of Bath had lived so long surrounded by the bomb-sites of 1942 that they had ceased to be the raw horrors they once had been and were now just walked past more-or-less un-noticed, having mellowed into commonplace features of the city that may have always been there.

The one factor above all others that threw the Luftwaffe's depredations into the shadows of history, however, was the City Council's systematic and unforgiveable destruction of the working-class foothills of Georgian Bath during the 1960s and 1970s. It is widely believed that the so-called 'Sack of Bath' that saw the destruction of huge swathes of perfectly serviceable Georgian artisan's housing was an unavoidable consequence of the post-war rebuilding of bomb-damaged areas of the city. This, however, is far from the truth. The wholesale destruction of much of Georgian Bath was planned long before the war as part of a city-wide slum clearance scheme. The appalling state of Britain's working class housing stock, not just in the larger industrial cities but also in seemingly quaint country market towns, was a pre-war national scandal and one which, by 1939, was finally being addressed by local and national government. The Second World War temporarily placed this process in abeyance. By 1948, however, every city or town in England of any size had prepared rose-tinted plans for development, redevelopment or civic improvement, few of which were practicable and fewer still of which were implemented. Bath was one of the exceptions and here the city planners tore through the supposedly, but not actually, unfit artisan enclaves with almost messianic ruthlessness. The scale of destruction was such that it achieved national notoriety. Eventually public outrage, voiced through the press, brought the onslaught on Bath's priceless Georgian heritage under control and, on a wider canvas, forced a more rational approach to post-war development nationwide. The consequence of the blunders of the city planners and of the city architect's department was that all the architectural woes of Bath were laid at their doors; the infamy of the 1960s swamped and virtually obliterated all recollection of the damage inflicted by the Luftwaffe in 1942.

When *The Bombing of Bath* was first published in 1983 it went some way towards redressing the balance, but popular interest in Second World War history was not, perhaps, as intense then as it is now a quarter of a century on and the book did not quite achieve the recognition it undoubtedly deserved. Today, though, interest in all aspects of Britain's social history is greater, more sustained and more sophisticated than it has ever been, due largely to the plethora of populist television history programmes and the accessibility to original sources offered by the internet. In this context this book stands as the definitive account of a key period in the history of Bath, now a World Heritage City, and is a book that will never be eclipsed. Niall Rothnie's research is a perfect synthesis of official documentary evidence, newspaper reports and first-hand oral accounts of men and women who witnessed the events of April 1942. It is the careful blending, comparison and cross-checking of information about the same events from disparate sources that has ensured the consistent accuracy of Niall's work. Historians are aware that no single account of any event can be relied upon: official documents may recount the facts but are often infuriatingly sparse and often biased to reflect the requirements of the department that originated them; newspaper reports, especially in wartime, are almost invariably disingenuous, propagandist and frequently censored, while personal recollections are all too often distorted by the passage of time. Where such recollections can be substantiated by supporting sources they can be truly invaluable; they add flesh to the skeleton of documentary evidence, they are totally immersive and can place the reader in the heart of the action. Reliable oral history, well written, is the literary equivalent of audio surround-sound. And this, of course, is an asset that will largely be denied to future historians because, as the war recedes further into history there are, quite literally, fewer and fewer survivors left to tell the tale.

Finally, though, a word of warning to budding authors and historians upon the pitfalls of over reliance on personal recollections: sometimes they are completely wrong! Shortly after our *Bath Blitz* exhibition was opened at Monkton Farleigh Mine an old chap, a life-long resident of Bath, commented:

> *'Well, it's a really interesting display, the pictures are excellent but you know, don't you, that you've got the facts completely wrong? The bombing was in 1943, not 1942.'*

We assured him that we had researched the subject pretty carefully and that all the major institutions from the *Evening Chronicle* to the Imperial War Museum seemed to agree with us. He was quite adamant however:

> *'No,'* he said, *'I know it was 1943 because my daughter was married in April 1943 and the bombing happened on the weekend of her wedding.'*

There was really no arguing with that, so the conversation ended in a state of stubborn stalemate. Perhaps he was right all along and this entire book is based on a wholly erroneous premise ...

Nick McCamley
Monkton Farleigh
January 2010

Acknowledgements

My chief debt is to those whose memories constitute the bulk of this book: it would be invidious to single out any particular contributor and I am glad to be able to list all their names. Other sources have given me much help, in particular Mr. R Bryant, the Bath City Archivist; the staff of Bath Reference Library; and the staff of the Imperial War Museum.

Finally I must record my thanks for help of a more personal nature: Mr. J P Wroughton and Mr. R J Rowe who helped me to start this project; Mr. J Graham Brown who helped me to finish it; and my wife and my mother who encouraged me throughout.

Niall Rothnie
1983

Publisher's acknowledgement

We would like to record our special thanks to Mr. Jim Warren and the Bath Blitz Memorial Project for providing additional photographic illustrations for this new edition.

Contents

Chapter		Page
1	Preparations in Peacetime	1
2	The First Years of the War	9
3	Bath the Target	15
4	The German View of the Raids: First Night	21
5	Saturday Night: The First Raid	31
6	Saturday: Raid Two	43
7	Sunday	61
8	Sunday: Raid Three	79
9	Monday	95
10	The First Week	113
11	Clearing Up	137
	Postscript	157
	Bibliography	169
	Index	171

CHAPTER ONE

Preparations in Peacetime

Of all the cities attacked during the so-called 'Baedeker' raids in early 1942, Bath was the one that attracted the most attention. King George VI was outraged. It was widely suggested that by bombing an historic Roman city such as Bath, the Germans had once more shown their hatred for culture as well as human life. The fact that Bath was also a Georgian city seemed to rub further salt into the wound. For this was a period when men had supposedly been at their most cultured and sophisticated. Rumours abounded concerning assumed destruction. A contemporary history bemoaned the loss of great Roman relics. Various crescents, it appeared, had been totally demolished. In fact the ruin of historical areas was greatly exaggerated. Even so, the one major loss, the Assembly Rooms, received much publicity. One abiding image of the raids is that of a decidedly battered sedan chair standing amid piles of gutted rubble that had once been the Assembly Rooms.

To understand why the raids caused so much consternation, it is necessary to go back a few years before 1942. A very few German aircraft carrying a very few bombs had created a number of casualties and a great deal of worry in London in the latter part of World War I. Theorists between the wars had used these meagre statistics to put forward scenarios of total aerial devastation in any future conflict. They took a pessimistic viewpoint. They assumed that on the outbreak of war the whole German air force might head immediately for London; that all would get through; that all bombs would hit their targets; that this onslaught might be maintained for at least two weeks. Assuming all this, it was widely believed that key centres of industry and population would be systematically devastated within days of the declaration of war. Millions of panic-stricken Londoners were expected to flee the smoking remains of their city to seek refuge elsewhere, leaving hundreds of thousands behind, dead.

It never quite happened that way, of course. But to prepare for the worst, the government had, before the war started, divided the country into areas or zones of probability: which areas would and which would not be expected to suffer air raids. The big cities were in the first category as centres of industry and trade, and therefore prime targets. In these areas, great encouragement was given to non-essential personnel – young children in particular, to be evacuated to safer areas. This often meant the rural west of England which was relatively distant from the Luftwaffe and from its assumed targets.

Bath itself was a key centre for evacuation. One must remember that the great air attacks were expected as soon as the war began; so on the last day before hostilities broke out, September 2, 1939, at least 4,000 evacuees arrived by train at Bath. Some were billeted in the city but most used the railway as the quickest way out of London prior to being spread throughout Somerset. Many more arrived in the following days, the vast majority coming from the East End of London. By the end of 1939 it was reckoned that the population of Bath had increased by a massive ten thousand, to a new high of just under eighty thousand. Many adults were also exercising, as they saw it, proper caution in moving to the West Country. Although this was by no means the whole truth, the charge that Bath was a 'city of old crocks', people living out the war in some comfort and with little care for others not so fortunate, was one repeatedly levelled by some of the national press throughout the war. A small minority, as ever, gave a bad name to the rest.

One group of evacuees stood out as being different. This was the Admiralty. To be accurate, a number of important government departments were moved down to, and around, Bath. It held a number of attractions. The Bath stone underground quarries had been worked for a number of centuries and as a result, within a triangle based on Bath, Bradford-on-Avon to the south and Corsham to the east, there were vast man-made caverns. These were safe from attack themselves and in an area that was itself presumed safe from attack. As early as 1934 a government tour of England looking for suitable underground stores for munitions and explosives had earmarked both the Corsham-Box complex and the quarries at Bradford-on-Avon for future use. By 1938 the international situation had grown more tense. The government had taken over the vast underground site at Eastlays to the south of Corsham. It also had Monkton Farleigh, a large site under the hill above the village of Bathford. This was only a few miles from the centre of Bath. Under the ground, around Brown's Folly, the old mining chambers were straightened and levelled, conveyor belts, vehicles and equipment brought in. By 1940 a huge collection of essential goods was in burrows to the east and south of Bath. Near Corsham were Ministry of Supply ordnance stores along with one of the largest underground aircraft factories in the country. At the Westwood quarry near Bradford-on-Avon there were engineering works and a store of British Museum treasures. At Monkton Farleigh was another large store of munitions. Although these were underground, documents from the period cast doubts on the supposed advantages of such shelters. They stress the fact that these quarries were temporary stores of arms; and that a serious air attack could penetrate, cause a massive explosion and severely damage surrounding property. This is an interesting point, as during the Bath raids many people took shelter in the area above Bathford to avoid danger. As it is, there is no evidence to suggest that the Germans knew anything of these stores. Certainly they never really dropped bombs in the area. From above, all that could be seen was a collection of guard-houses, ventilation plant and entrances to the shafts; plus a rather large number of pillboxes.

The Admiralty personnel were another matter; their existence was known of by the Nazi high command. Once again preparations for a move had long preceded the start of the war. Non-essential women and children were moved; the Admiralty applied this idea to their own operations. They had long planned to send their administrative sections to somewhere outside of London. A suitable site would be within easy reach of the capital, perhaps 50-100 miles away and on a major railway line. Bath cropped up as a possible site at least as early as 1938. Few personnel were told until the last moment, with inevitable rumour and confusion resulting. At the time of the Munich crisis in September 1938, Walter Sweetenham remembers his father being told that they would be going to Reading. When the war did start William Burden found his office in London being told on alternate days that they were, and then were not moving. Hubert Jackson, working in Whitehall, received one day's notice before being sent to Bath. All personnel had to leave their families behind. They were warned not to make any commitments as regards staying in Bath; they might be on the move again.

Even without their families, the Admiralty's arrival had greatly increased the accommodation problem. Although specialised hutments were soon going up at Foxhill, the main offices were in large buildings in the centre of the city. Some were requisitioned schools and colleges. The Admiralty also made use of some of the grandest hotels. If the key works were still in London, some important sites were in Bath. A document listing places requiring protection against air attack lists all four Admiralty requisitioned hotels: the Pump Room, Pulteney, Spa and Empire. These were category A, vital bases, the destruction of which would be considered a 'disaster'. After the Bath raids, German radio was to make much play of the destruction of 'High British staffs' in their hotels in the centre of the city. In fact, none of the Admiralty buildings received major damage. That the accusation was made at all is interesting. It is an irony that the Admiralty had moved to Bath in part because it was not an obvious target; but by doing so they had increased the likelihood that the city might become a target. The point was made later. The then commander of the British anti-aircraft defence, General Pile, admitted that Bath perhaps should have been provided with some degree of active defence. Apart from the Admiralty, Bath also had a number of industries geared to war. Stothert & Pitt produced components for tanks, and other war equipment. Perhaps this is a valid point, but it is being wise after the event. As we see, any town however beautiful and unwarlike, can usually be found to possess some minor activity or industry that can qualify it for an attack.

Bath was not completely unwarlike; nor was it completely undefended. With equipment in short supply she had no barrage balloons nor any permanent anti-aircraft batteries. The only obvious signs of defence were the two airfields on the hills near the city: Colerne and its satellite Charmy Down. They were primarily for the defence of Bristol. Neither was ready for the start of the war. Colerne became operational in January 1940 with the black-painted Hurricanes of 87 Squadron the first unit to be based there. Charmy Down opened at the end of the same year and in the following summer received the Defiants of 125 Squadron. Both squadrons, for all their enthusiasm, were handicapped by a lack of modern aircraft and any real means of detecting the enemy in the dark. These were also the two squadrons guarding Bath when it was attacked in 1942.

This relative lack of active defences is quite understandable considering that period. Equipment was scarce. It was still felt that the enemy would only attack the larger towns. The only danger was that an occasional stray bomb might land on Bath, one meant for elsewhere. It was expected that bombers heading for Bristol, a port and centre of aircraft production, might hit the wrong target by accident. Otherwise, as did happen, they might jettison bombs in order to escape from fighter attack. This, Bath's Civil Defence organisation could cope with. To quote Major Geoffrey Lock, who was largely responsible for arranging the system,

> We didn't know what we were planning, but we didn't anticipate we would get what we did ... I didn't expect Bath to be blitzed, except for the odd bomb.

As long ago as 1935, the government had suggested that local councils begin to think of some form of civil defence. By the outbreak of war, Bath had created such a system, capable of dealing with the occasional bomb.

It also fitted into a national network that could provide

additional support should the unthinkable happen and Bath be the sole object of an enemy attack. The system was modified during the war but in essence remained the same. Radar would detect an approaching enemy air attack. Once its direction had been assessed, the towns that might be bombed sounded their sirens, at which point everyone was meant to take cover. For most, at home, this meant one of the mass-produced family shelters: the Anderson in the garden or the Morrison indoors. If they had neither, then they used the cupboard under the stairs as the safest refuge. Most advice claimed it was best to stay put and in the open; the council provided a varied group of public shelters. Most parks had their half-sunk shelter. In the centre of the city, church crypts were often strengthened. Many could hold two hundred: the largest shelter at North Parade could hold four times as many. More numerous were the brick-built oblong shelters at the side of many roads. Some of the first were viewed with suspicion as being badly constructed. No shelter in fact was proof against a direct hit; but many preferred the feeling of greater safety and of being with other people that the public shelters provided. Knowing one's nearest refuge was considered essential by many. The Scala cinema in Oldfield Park reassured its patrons by advertising the fact that there were two brand new shelters directly opposite.

Assume then that a few stray bombs had fallen on Bath. The 'incident' would be located by the local warden or policeman who would make two telephone calls. One would be to the Fire Service, the other to Bath Civil Defence control centre. This was first located at the central police station in the Orange Grove. Soon after the war started it moved to the basement of Apsley House in Lower Weston. Here were the organisation's senior officers, a whole range of telephone and messenger facilities and representatives from all the major services: police, fire, medicine, and also gas, electricity and the Admiralty. As incidents were reported, each representative would decide what he needed to provide as assistance. The main units involved were medical and rescue. There were a number of first aid party depots equipped also with ambulances. These were assisted at incidents by the rescue squads, a mixture of first aiders and building experts. Such men would know how to get casualties out of wrecked buildings. Once casualties had been located, a rough assessment was made of the seriousness of their injuries. The ambulances would take the lightly injured to first aid posts, the badly hurt straight to hospital; and the dead to the emergency mortuaries. Those that were bombed out but uninjured were taken to various halls designated as rest centres.

The whole system placed a great strain on resources. Obviously key fire and medical personnel were professionals. Many were unpaid volunteers though, who had to cope with a full time job as well as eight-hour stints every two or three nights at a first aid post, for example. With most able-bodied men conscripted, a large number of personnel were women. Leslie Nott, who helped organise the messenger service, often had those who were under or over age, the unfit, those in protected occupations, conscientious objectors. The equipment was equally diverse. Temporary ambulances were often converted vans. The Fire Service received the strangest equipment of all. Requisitioned coal and fruit lorries carried pumps. Trailer pumps were towed by an assortment of taxis, lorries and even a hearse.

No vehicle carried a wireless; once an incident had been cleared up the ambulance driver would report back to his depot. If the telephone system was disrupted by bombing, a motorbike and bicycle messenger service would operate. If Apsley House was hit there was an alternative control centre. In reality this comprised a few telephones in a bowling alley at the Foresters Arms at Foxhill. The Civil Defence depots were many and scattered. They were often on the outskirts of the city to avoid a knock-out blow. Not all were ideally placed. The main Rescue Party depot was near the Midland Bridge. This was an unpopular choice as there was only one narrow entrance. 'It was like a gas trap; there were gasometers nearby.' If Bath felt it had too much to cope with, it could call in assistance from outside. This was a provision that was to prove very useful later on.

Once the war began, a number of changes were made. In particular Fire Guards were provided to watch at night for incendiaries in churches, factories and other untenanted buildings. But these were in the future and the system just described was that with which Bath faced the coming of war in late 1939.

CHAPTER TWO

The First Years of the War

The war came to Bath on September 2nd, 1939: but a war of announcements and proclamations rather than of actual fighting. Lists were published telling people the location of their nearest first aid post and fire station. Appeals were made for army recruits, blood donors and sandbag fillers. The long awaited bombing campaign might start at any time. The shelters were opened for use. Places of public entertainment such as the Assembly Rooms were closed down lest a bomb hit them when they were packed with people. In Batheaston there was a minor panic when a sharp bang led to fear of a bomb attack. It turned out to be a tyre bursting.

There were no greater alarms that day, nor the next when war was actually declared; nor for the rest of 1939. As Poland was crushed by Germany, England and France could only watch as their armies were mobilised. The Royal Air Force (RAF) dropped only leaflets for fear of massive German retaliation. Only at sea did a full-scale war develop and the local newspapers reflected this in occasional reports. Nine local men were reported drowned in HMS *Courageous*. Bath's interest in the battle of the River Plate was increased by the news that not only was there a Bath man serving on HMS *Exeter*, but another had been held captive on the scuttled German ship, the *Graf Spee*.

These were remote incidents. The much-feared air bombardment did not materialise but it was still felt that London might be attacked and the refugees continued to arrive in Bath. A Mrs. Potter, then a child, remembers seeing a crocodile of evacuees from London walking from the railway station to St. Mark's School. Many were dirty and scruffy. Some had to be deloused. Mrs. Potter made friends with a young German Jewess. The girl told many stories of what it was like to be a Jew in central Europe at that time. Mrs. Potter listened politely, but 'we didn't really believe her at the time, as we were only children'. The war was naturally even more remote for the young. Walter Sweetenham, who was a pupil at the City of

Bath Boys' School, remembers periodic gasmask inspections. There was a drill whereby if the sirens sounded an alert, most of the pupils had to run to designated houses in adjacent roads to take shelter. This procedure provided a welcome relief from school for Dorothy Smith, then at Bathwick School. It was a source of much amusement to the children if not to the receiving householders. Dorothy Smith's parents were not happy at the idea that she should take cover in the public shelter in Henrietta Park as it was considered too close to Admiralty buildings for comfort. Later on, frequent alarms led to the abandonment of this scheme. It became too disruptive and the schools themselves were strengthened as shelters. At the City of Bath Boys' School the area under the gymnasium was given additional supports and sandbagged. This was in the future though. In 1939 the only real disruption was caused by the influx of refugees into Bath schools, leading to '40 plus in not very large classrooms'.

The East End evacuees were sometimes dirty and smelly. They were not always welcomed with open arms by some of the inhabitants of Bath. Away from home and family, it could not be said that all the evacuees enjoyed their new surroundings either. This applied with equal vigour to both young and old. The newly arrived Admiralty staff had been told to travel on their own, and as a result many spent a miserable Christmas 1939, one of the coldest on record, crammed together in freezing and decidedly substandard flats. Not only did they add further to the overcrowding in Bath, but also the Admiralty paid the landlords a derisory guinea a week for bed and board, thus earning the men the name of 'guinea pigs'. A correspondence developed in some local papers between disgruntled Bathonians complaining about poor money paid by the new arrivals, and Admiralty men complaining about the poor reception they were receiving. The Admiralty continued to stress that no commitments should be made. Most decided, rightly, to ignore this ruling. William Burden brought his family down in March 1940 by which time Walter Sweetenham's father had been long settled in Keynsham with his family, while commuting to the Pump Room Hotel each day.

The Admiralty staff brought their families to them. As the air raids on London did not occur, many other evacuees went back to their families in the capital. The Civil Defence services were ready and waiting. They spent most of their time waiting. Marjorie Horsell spent her long hours on duty knitting sea-boot stockings, training volunteers and checking the equipment. One first aider used his ambulance not for bomb victims, but for taking nurses to hospital, and drinks to the police. As usual, when services are created but not used, criticism soon came. A fire officer, Herbert Bath, remembers his men being called 'part time dart players'. The shelters opened but, unused, had their own difficulties. A number were vandalised.

Yet by mid-summer 1940 the situation seemed to have changed beyond all recognition. Hitler had struck against the west in May and, within two months, France had been defeated and the Battle of Britain had begun. The Luftwaffe now threatened England, at last, with continued air raids. There was even the threat of actual invasion. The Home Guard was formed. Admiralty personnel found themselves crawling through fields on manoeuvres and guarding the mouths of various railway tunnels. The Admiralty thought of taking further appropriate measures against attack. A survey found they possessed only ten Lewis machine-guns for road block defences around Bath. There was a plan to set up anti-aircraft (AA) machine-guns on top of all major Admiralty buildings in Bath. On the Holburne of Menstrie museum, guns would ward off dive-bombers flying along the wide expanse of Pulteney Street. But the plan came to nothing; and dive-bombers never used that route.

Now the 'blitz' had started in the capital, the evacuees came back to Bath and brought new experiences to the city, as Doris Smith recalls:

Once when I was driving an ambulance the siren went and I told some children to take cover as they were still playing in the street. One of them said to me 'Cor Blimey miss, we had worse than this in London'. I felt that small.

In fact, most people in Bath were becoming accustomed to paying little attention to the air raid sirens despite, by now, the occasional bomb. One of the first landed near Bath on August 24th, 1940: it killed a rook. A spate of bombs in the first week of September damaged a road junction, a couple of houses and Bath City football ground. One pony was killed, two people were injured. There were still no deaths and Bath's continued immunity brought forward a number of strange explanations. It was believed by some that the city was in a valley too narrow for bombers to fly down. The local paper carried a report that a captured German pilot had said he would never raid Bath as he had many friends there. There was a scattering of high-explosive bombs in Bath in the last months of 1940 when the Luftwaffe made a series of attacks on Bristol and elsewhere. These did nothing to dent morale as they damaged a number of properties but harmed no one.

Bristol suffered a succession of 29 raids between November 1940 and July of the following year. Bath's proximity to Bristol meant that she received a large number of false alerts. There were so many that on the night of the 16th January, 1941, Bath received its 400th alert. Few paid any real attention. However, this one was different. Above the city, a lone German bomber, desperately trying to evade a British night fighter, jettisoned its mixture of high-explosives and incendiaries. The incendiaries fell across Englishcombe Lane and were speedily extinguished, but for once, not all the high-explosive bombs landed in waste ground. The first came down upon two houses in Twerton High Street, one of which was empty. In the second there were four children, the eldest thirteen. They were the Randell family who had been evacuated from London at the very start of the war. Three were killed outright, the fourth suffered fractured ribs and both arms were broken. Outside in the street two men were cut down and killed by flying fragments from the same explosion.

Another bomb from the same stick landed outside West Twerton School. A bloke came out of his house, turned and was hit by a piece of metal in his neck. We picked him up in the 'dead box', a box with four stretchers. We got a bad report; someone said he wasn't dead but this was untrue as he had shrapnel in his head.

(Don Tuddenham, ambulance driver)

The last victim was taken to the hospital, the other five to St. Peter's Church mortuary in Twerton. They were the first fatalities in Bath, three of them children who had been sent by well-meaning parents away from just such a danger.

On Good Friday, April 11th, Bristol received another raid. By midnight the attack had finished and the 'all clear' had been sounded. Then, just afterwards, another lone German aircraft flew over Bath and dropped three or four bombs on the Dolemeads area of Widcombe. A Mr. Jackson, a police officer, was one of the first on the scene:

I was on my way to the control point at the bottom of Widcombe Hill when a 'plane came over. I heard three bombs drop and saw a great sheet of flame go up. The bomb had hit the gas main. I went to the scene of where the bombs had dropped. People were milling around. Some were crying, some were shocked. A warden said to me that there were houses down and casualties. He said he had seen some lying in the road and he thought the gas and water mains had gone. I went to my nearest telephone and rang the central police station ... there were about eleven dead I think.

Some records say ten died, some say eleven. Another who heard the bombs was Edwin Stainer, a schoolboy then:

I was in bed at the time. I heard some hollow sounding bangings. They were loud — about a couple of hundred yards away. I got up, tore downstairs and got under the table and stayed there. Next day I went out and saw the scene. Everyone was struck silent.

There was a footnote to this raid. Eight of the dead were taken to the mortuary at St. James' Church where they were left unattended. The next day, Saturday, the verger was distressed to find that three people had got into the crypt 'to see the bodies'. Seven of them were soon removed but by some oversight the final body was left there for over a week, without a coffin. It gave off an odour which was soon noticed by the congregation in the church above.

CHAPTER THREE

Bath the Target

Bath had been, so far, only an accidental target. It is now necessary to look at why Bath became a planned one.

The German air offensive came almost to a halt at the end of spring 1942, as the bulk of the Luftwaffe was transferred to the Eastern front for the invasion of Russia. The Western front became something of a backwater. It had few aircraft, especially modern ones. The crews were often newly trained or those starting again after a lay-off caused by injury. The western air fleet, Luftflotte III, therefore could make only limited attacks. It made reconnaissance patrols, laid mines and made the occasional attack on shipping. Hitler was holding on in the west but doing little else there; nor was he keeping resources in the west that could do much more.

From now on, it was the RAF that put more bombers over enemy territory at night. In fact, Bomber Command had been active since the start of the war, but with relatively little success. By early 1942, for many reasons, success had become imperative. A number of the British air staff had begun the war with the belief that Bomber Command could bomb the enemy into submission without the need for any other assistance. No invasion of Europe would be necessary. The shell-shocked Germans would surrender and the army would just be sent in as a policing force. This rather extreme view was never fully endorsed by the Prime Minister, Churchill, but he had no real alternative. After Dunkirk and Britain's retreat from mainland Europe, the bomber offensive was the only real contribution that Britain could make to the war. It had to be effective.

Unfortunately, in the early years of the war, this was not the case. The available bombers were too small. Daytime bombing was too costly in terms of aircraft lost. Night-time attacks were notoriously inaccurate but the only real alternative. However, if Germany was to be raided at night, then this posed a great moral problem. It was generally accepted that one should bomb only military targets. The British had begun the war by being careful about what they bombed. Indeed, if target warships were too close to shore then the bombers were instructed to bring their bombs home rather than risk killing German civilians. By 1941 such niceties were no longer observed by either side. The British theorised. Factories were legitimate targets but they could not be pinpointed in the dark. The only way to destroy them was to drop bombs throughout the city in which they were situated. Such indiscriminate bombing would naturally kill some civilians, but some of them might be factory workers. Actually to admit to the deliberate killing of civilians was going a little too far and Air Ministry directives stressed that the attacks were on enemy morale. The worker would be depressed at the destruction of his home and not turn up for work. The point that he might be destroyed along with his home was not emphasised.

This policy was tacitly accepted throughout 1941; and still Bomber Command could not deliver the goods. Critics became vocal. There were demands that Bomber Command's aircraft should be sent to theatres where they could be of more use; the desert war in North Africa for example. Bomber Command replied by increasing their own demands. They wanted 4,000 bombers and then they could win the war on their own. However, this would use much of the country's industrial capacity, and leave little to develop other weapons systems; and, said the critics, what proof was there that any use of a bomber offensive could achieve success?

At this low point in Bomber Command's fortunes they began, at last, to receive the equipment they needed. Bigger four-engined bombers such as the Lancaster began to enter service. A new navigation aid, code-named *Gee*, was available for more accurate night-bombing. On the 14th February, 1942 a new Air Ministry directive spelled out what had been vaguely accepted before. It gave the go-ahead for a full-scale bombing offensive directed against the morale of enemy industrial workers. Thus, when a new commander-in-chief of Bomber Command, Harris, took over a week later, he had the equipment and the permission. All that he needed was to prove the value of the aircraft under his command.

On the 3rd March an attack was made on an arms works in Paris; a dangerous target if the accuracy was poor. British records claimed a high degree of accuracy, but hundreds of French civilians appear to have been killed. Hitler was furious. He demanded an immediate reprisal raid on a British target. That the German leader could get worked up about French losses may seem strange, but it was one way to engender anti-British feeling in France. Even more important, this had been a major attack by British forces after a winter lull and Germany must be seen able to respond to such provocation.

Yet only a few days later Hitler cancelled the idea of a punitive raid. He gave his reasons to Jeschonnek, his Luftwaffe Chief of Staff. He admitted that with the present aircraft in the west he could not mete out appropriately heavy raids on British cities. Such a raid might provoke a further British response, and next time a German rather than a French town might be the target. The British were not coming to Germany in great numbers, so why encourage them? Soon after there were a couple of scattered raids on Kiel and Essen in Germany itself. They were not successful enough to change Hitler's views.

Harris was still looking for the one successful raid to prove the effectiveness of Bomber Command. On the night of the 28th March, Bomber Command struck at the Baltic port of Lübeck. This had featured in the February directive, if rather low down on the list of targets, as an 'alternative target' because it was a port and had a handful of industries producing war materiels. Most urban areas can be found to possess some legitimate target, though. In this case there were other less moral advantages. The official RAF historians described Lübeck as 'operationally vulnerable', a vague phrase. It meant that the crowded wooden houses of the medieval Hanseatic town would burn easily. Harris wrote that Lübeck was 'built more like a fire-lighter than a human habitation', and that the raid was a test. It was a number of tests in fact. It would show whether a town could be destroyed by incendiary bombs. It would show whether an attack could be concentrated in such a short time that it could overwhelm the fire services. It would try to time a record raid so as to catch as many of the rescue services as possible. However, it was also a demonstration. Harris was proving to his critics that Bomber Command could, as it had always claimed, destroy cities. To make sure, his first was an easy target, a small rather beautiful city that would catch fire quickly.

By any standards, the raid was a success. Perhaps 40-50% of Lübeck was destroyed by fire. The medieval centre, the Altstadt, went up in smoke. Among the buildings turned to ash were most of the merchants' timbered houses, the market hall and the Cathedral. Goebbels, the German propaganda minister, was most worried at the scale of the destruction. Hitler was irate. His previous desire to avoid massive attacks on Germany had failed. Now, instead of one reprisal attack, he decided on a whole series of raids on the principle, as he saw it, that the British had used. There would be surprise attacks on undefended, historic towns that had not been attacked before. The Air Staff agreed. Undefended, small towns were the most that the depleted forces of Luftflotte III could cope with. The Naval Staff protested that it meant taking aircraft away from what they saw as the essential task of hitting Britain's sea communications. They were ignored. On the 14th April, Hitler issued the official order to the Luftwaffe, openly demanding 'terror attacks of a retaliatory nature'. This was probably the first time that any war leader had admitted, if only to his own staff, that he was bombing to cause panic and not to hit vague industrial targets.

The British had few inklings that a new German offensive was imminent. In March only a score or so people had died in Britain from isolated bomb attacks. The very day that Lübeck was hit, British intelligence noted that a number of Luftwaffe units were moving west from the Netherlands into France. By the 2nd April this movement was so pronounced that it was being commented upon. The wrong conclusions were made. The Germans were either going for more reconnaissance patrols or anti-shipping attacks.

Then, on the nights of the 23rd/24th and 24/25th April,

two scattered raids were made on Exeter and the surrounding region. Neither was particularly successful and on the third night the Luftwaffe went for a new target.

CHAPTER FOUR

The German View of the
Raids: First Night

On the night of the 25th April, 1942 the weather over most of Europe was near perfect. There was a good moon, clear visibility and only a few clouds. At this stage of the war it meant that conditions favoured the attack. With airborne radar still in its infancy, good visibility helped the bomber seeking its target rather than the fighter looking for the bomber. It became dark around 9.00 pm. 128 aircraft from Bomber Command took off from airfields in the east of England for a third consecutive attack on the Baltic port of Rostock. It was their most successful attack yet on the city. At the same time a dozen German bombers were flying over the North Sea to make a raid on north-east Scotland. They made several hits on a factory in Aberdeen. They flattened a fair number of tenements nearby and caused a handful of casualties before returning home. It was a nuisance raid and evaluated as such by the home defences.

In north-west France the weather was not so good. In heavy skies and some rain 163 German bombers were preparing for the main attack of the night. It was to be the biggest German effort in almost a year. To make an attack on such a scale had not proved easy for the Luftwaffe High Command. Most of their aircraft were relatively old and slow. There were relatively few of the more modern Dornier Do.217. Many had only just been moved to France. The crews also left much to be desired. It was later estimated that at least one third of the aircraft involved came from Reserve Training Units. Luftflotte III was a danger, but not all-powerful.

From around 9.30 pm onwards, the bombers began to take off. There was the 4th Gruppe of KG2, only recently arrived in France, KG30 from the Netherlands, KG4, and KG55. There was the newly trained 1st Gruppe of KG2 equipped with Do.217's and KG106 with venerable Junkers Ju.88's. From Bruselis/Evere came more Ju.88's from KG3. Leading them all was Reconnaissance Gruppe 123 from Lanion, skilled pathfinders who would drop the first flares on the target.

The target was Bath. The German orders make it clear that this was the only target and the aim one of 'retribution' for the British attacks on the cultured cities of Lübeck and Rostock. The plan was a copy of recent British tactics in other ways as well. In theory, a massed bomber stream would make a concentrated attack to overwhelm the Civil Defence services. The Germans had long possessed a variety of radio beams to guide their aircraft to the target. The British had long since learned how to jam each successive beam by sending out identical signals. The Germans had recently introduced a supersonic frequency, one above human hearing, into their radio signals. Once again, the British had found this out. However, a mistake had been made. The new British listening receivers were wrongly redesigned. As the first bombers took off and fixed onto the radio signals, known as *X-Taub*, the British jammers were monitoring the signals; but their new sets could not receive the supersonic frequency, and nothing registered. As a result, the signals were not jammed and a number of inexperienced German crews must have found their way when otherwise they might have got lost.

Just after 10.15 pm the first bombers crossed the south coast of England on a broad front from Devon to the Isle of Wight. A German reporter, who claimed to be in one of the aircraft, gave the following account:

Late in the evening of the 25th April, many German bombers took off and approached their target through banks of clouds. On the British coast the first searchlights flashed up. The Tommies don't yet know where the bombers are heading; they feel secure.

This was true: the British did not know where they were heading. After two successive attacks on Exeter, the expert crews of 307 (Polish) night-fighter squadron were patrolling above that city. Elsewhere, there were a few odd aircraft up on training and exercise missions: nothing more. As the Germans crossed the coast, the AA guns opened up. Portland began firing at 10.27 pm. They made no impression. As the aircraft flew over Dorset in the general direction of Bath, the two local squadrons, 87 and 125, put up aircraft from Colerne and Charmy Down, respectively.

At one minute before eleven, the red raider-imminent-warning was given to Bath and the sirens sounded. Already the first bombers had arrived overhead; but a number flew on and beyond, towards Bristol. The AA guns there went into action at 10.55 pm. Even today, it is still thought that Bristol was a joint target. Yet the German instructions specify that it was a revenge raid 'on Bath, near Bristol'. There, perhaps, lies the answer. Later German radio broadcasts said that Bath was situated 'south-east of Bristol on the Avon'. It was natural that largely untrained crews, looking for a large town on the river Avon, might hit the wrong one. This possibility is encouraged by the fact that the bombs that hit Bristol were concentrated on the eastern quarter of the city; that is to say the side nearer Bath. Bristol attracted relatively few of the raiders but they did cause some confusion to both sides.

Meanwhile, the attack on the true target was developing apace. Despite later assertions, and hopes, of German planners, the raid was not a short, concentrated one. The 'bomber stream' did not materialise and the hoped for 30 minute attack stretched into a two hour one, and a very uneven one at that. Once the bombers arrived over Bath, the clear skies and bright moon provided good visibility. Without AA protection or adequate night-fighter cover, Bath was subjected to a terrifying ordeal. German aircraft flew around at will, taking their time before dropping their bomb loads. Some, for good measure, continued overhead and machine-gunned the streets below to discourage the Civil Defence workers rather than to cause actual damage and injury.

The fighters of 87 and 125 Squadrons were over Bath as well; but to little avail. As a ministry report commented ruefully later, these squadrons were supposed to compensate for the lack of AA guns in the area. No one had expected a full-scale attack like this. Despite the enthusiasm of the pilots, their equipment was quite simply not up to it. 87 Squadron was still using the Hurricane, a useful daytime fighter but of little use at night. The aircraft had their own inbuilt radar to track down the enemy. They had an early mark of this AI (Airborne Interception) device which had very limited range and was notoriously unreliable. The squadron had the further misfortune of having to operate in fighter boxes – a set area for each aircraft to patrol, which largely failed to coincide with the route the bombers took. The AI radar failed to make contacts although the frustrated pilots could sometimes see Germans, however briefly. Intermittent light and the often superior speed of the German bombers prevented effective pursuit. The only loss of the evening over Bath was, in fact, one of 87's Hurricanes. A Pilot Officer McNair ran out of fuel on his main tanks. He tried to restart his engine, was pursued by a German, still failed to get his engine working and had to bail out. He landed safely, though bruised.

Meanwhile, 125 Squadron from Charmy Down was having an equal lack of success. They started with what appeared to be an advantage. Only a few days before the raids, they had re-equipped with the better night-fighter, the Beaufighter. This had a much more advanced mark of the AI radar. A ground station, GCI (Ground Controlled Interception) would pick up contact on their radar and direct the fighter until it made contact with its AI. This would soon bring the crew within visual range and a 'kill' could then be made. However, a steady approach like this necessitated a steady flight by the opposition. The Germans proved unobliging. As they circled Bath in a random pattern they were frequently picked up by the Beaufighters' AIs and then lost as they dived or climbed. Despite its advances, the new mark AI still had its limitations. In particular it lost contact with aircraft when they dived low. The radar blip was lost in the reflection back from the ground. With the best will in the world, pilots in new and different aircraft also found it difficult to keep in contact with the enemy. By the end of the evening 125 Squadron had recorded numerous radar contacts, one visual and no combats.

The Germans roamed over Bath unhindered. The way in which they arrived, and flew around, makes it impossible to say where the first bombs landed. The first to be dropped were the flares of Reconnaissance Gruppe 123 as a guide to their less skilled colleagues following on behind. It is not obvious exactly what the Germans were aiming at in the half light of a 'bomber's moon'. The raid may have been a revenge one but either the attackers were very poor shots or they were not aiming specifically at Georgian Bath. The plot of bombs dropped suggests no particular pattern although a later German propaganda photograph seems to lay stress on the bombs that fell along the railway, bridges and the gasworks. It seems likely that the Luftwaffe command, on being told to plan an attack on Bath, took out a previous photographic plan of the city, which still exists, and worked from that. The plan, in common with all others of potential targets, laid stress on military-economic points. The gasworks figured prominently. They used this as a basis for their attack which they did not bother to adapt to 'cultural' targets. Nor would it have been very 'politique' in the world at large, to stress a desire to bomb non-military targets, whatever the true state of affairs.

Gunther Hoenicke, the war reporter previously mentioned, gives one account of the bombing:

> We swoop down from a high altitude and the first flares light the area. Below, the river Avon threads its way. The first small fires are already flaring. Suddenly, there is a huge darting flame – a gasometer has blown up. We descend further and see glowing houses beneath us. A black cloud of smoke hangs over the city: there is almost no wind. We can distinctly recognise the streets, and fires and destruction rage. Our observer calmly seeks a new target, dropping heavy bombs. More bombers approach and again and again there are explosions as one wave after another passes over the town, bringing death and destruction.

No German aircraft was lost over Bath that night. A number of light machine-guns opened fire from Colerne aerodrome itself at some aircraft that flew low. Despite optimistic claims, no real damage seems to have been caused. Elsewhere some successes were scored, though. At 11.05 pm Bristol AA claimed to have hit and damaged one of the raiders. As later aircraft crossed the coast, the by-now-alerted defences struck back. At 11.38 pm Portland AA destroyed an intruder, the first of the night. Further west, along the coast, the night-fighters were in action as well. 307 Squadron was already on patrol over Exeter. Not only was this an experienced squadron, it also had more experience than 125 Squadron with the Beaufighter. This gave results. Just south of Beer Head, Flight Lieutenant Neyder made contact at maximum range on his AI with an intruder. Unlike those over Bath, this one was flying straight and level. Within two minutes Neyder had seen his objective dead ahead. Closing to 200 yards he fired a short burst. A parachute appeared. The starboard tank caught fire. He fired again and the rest of the crew were seen to abandon the aircraft. The bomber, identified as a Ju.88, went down into the sea. Neyder was then directed by his ground station onto a second aircraft. This time he was seen and the raider took successful evasive action. A second 307 Squadron Beaufighter under Staff Sergeant Illasewicz made both AI and then visual contact with an incoming aircraft. A burst was seen to hit the raider and it dived towards the sea. It was claimed as a 'probable'. Both this Beaufighter and another, which made no contacts, flew on to land at Colerne.

These were the obvious successes. Others were less so. A Ju.88 of IV/KG3 had taken off at 9.36 pm but almost immediately had trouble with its direction-finding equipment. It was unable to follow the *X-Taub* radio signals, and by the time they reached England, the crew were hopelessly lost. Undaunted, they flew on; unknowingly, they flew well beyond Bath. Suddenly, at 11.30 pm, the aircraft was hit by a hail of bullets. The wireless operator was injured. The bombs were immediately jettisoned to increase the crew's chances of survival. They thought they had been hit by AA fire. In fact it was another night-fighter. Earlier in the evening a Beaufighter of 255 Squadron piloted by Pilot Officer Wyvill had taken off from High Ercall near Shrewsbury to practice with the new AI radar in conjunction with ground control (GCI) at Honiley. The practice became real when GCI picked up the lost Ju.88 and guided the Beaufighter onto it. By the time Wyvill had made visual contact both aircraft were over Hereford. After the first attack the raider took evasive action, swinging from port to starboard. Wyvill temporarily lost sight of his quarry. For a few minutes the Germans seemed safe but, unknown to them, Wyvill still had them on his radar. As the bomber levelled out again the fighter closed to within 50 yards, firing a four second burst. There were flashes all over the bomber. The starboard engine caught fire and the crew felt the aircraft begin to break up. It broke up too quickly for some. The already wounded wireless operator, along with the observer, managed to bail out; but the pilot and rear gunner were still in the aircraft when it went straight into a mountain below.

In a raid on Bath one would hardly expect to find an aircraft over Hereford. One had been found, only by luck, during a training flight.

Radio signals and skilled leaders could not help some of the less experienced bomber crews. The observer who survived from the ill-fated Hereford Ju.88 had been injured in Russia in 1941. This had been his first flight when fit again. The later British estimates were that 60-80 aircraft had made the main attack on Bath: an obvious underestimate. Yet many aircraft must have got lost. A number had gone on to Bristol by mistake. Other towns near Bath were bombed as well: Chippenham, for example, Keynsham, Trowbridge and Bradford-on-Avon. Other towns are less easily explained. How could Dorchester or Stroud be mistaken for Bath? All these were stray bombs. The only fatalities were at an even more unlikely location. This was Exeter, the target for the previous two nights. German bombers were recorded not only to and from Bath in the counties of Somerset, Dorset and Hampshire. They were even reported in Gloucester and South Wales.

The return to France was, therefore, a disorganised affair. Bombers returned at many different times. The final British success of this first raid came as the bombers began to return home. Once more it was a coincidence rather than a planned attack. Again it was a Beaufighter, this time from Tangmere in the south-east, and again it was on a practice test. Squadron Leader Topham was told of an aircraft approaching from the north-west on its way home. After a steady chase and the obligatory AI and then visual contact, Topham emptied his cannon and machine-guns into the luckless Do.17. It began to disintegrate as it banked steeply and down towards the sea.

This was the only aircraft lost on the return journey. The rest landed at their bases in Northern France; but the night was not yet over and many now began reloading for the second raid of the night. At least 40 bombers, probably more, took off again and crossed the French coast at around 4.00 am. As they reached the Isle of Wight the AA guns went into action. Portland at 4.22 am was the first. A second raid on Bath was not expected and once more the raiders imminent siren went as the bombers reached the city. The siren went at 4.35 am and at the same time Bristol AA opened fire. Five minutes later, the first aircraft of 87 Squadron took off. Neither they, nor 125 Squadron, had any more success now than before. More Germans were off-track. Detections were made in Wales and the Cardiff guns were in action briefly. As the raiders turned for home, the defences scored their only success. By this time of the night, no trainers were up. Between 5.18 and 5.22 am the Portsmouth defences fired a number of rockets and claimed to have damaged one aircraft. The alert remained in force in Bath until just after 6.00 am but by then most of the force had long gone. Only five tardy raiders were still in the Bristol and Swindon areas and they too soon left.

There was one other German loss that night. Unfortunately, the British records are often sparse and contradictory: no more so than in this case. One Do.217 came down near Wimborne in Dorset, but without the time being noted it is impossible to say why it came down. It might have been damaged by the AA guns of Bristol or Portsmouth; or possibly by one of 307 Squadron; or for another reason entirely.

By the end of the night, and allowing for the number of German raiders that had got lost on the way, it could be claimed a success for the attackers. Five had been destroyed. One was probably destroyed and at least two damaged. (This last was always a difficult thing to measure.) If we accept a minimum of 200 sorties, then enemy losses stood at a very low 21%. The British success seems even less impressive when one looks at the break-down. Of the five German aircraft shot down, two were by aircraft up on practice and a third by an aircraft that was patrolling Exeter. The technique of attacking new, undefended targets had clearly paid dividends for the Luftwaffe crews involved.

CHAPTER FIVE

Saturday Night: The First Raid

As on every other night, the Civil Defence services were ready for action. The ambulance depots were manned. First aid personnel were waiting. The wardens were coping with the daily problem of trying to keep track of people's movements. If a record was not kept, there would be no way of knowing how many casualties were inside a house should it be struck by a bomb. The Civil Defence organiser, Major Lock, had made a tour of wardens' posts. He jokingly reminded them to keep alert as a raid might come that very night. However, it was the weekend, and many more people were seeking some form of entertainment. In Oldfield Park, Sydney and Alma Poole of Second Avenue had gone to Mr. Poole's parents in nearby Stanley Road. Every Saturday they spent the evening playing whist. James Webster had gone to a variety show. As 11.00 pm approached, he was just going on fire-watching duty in Marlborough Lane.

Eric Davies was off-duty. He was on leave from the army. He should not, originally, have been home at this time but his pass had been brought forward when he fractured his wrist while playing football. Mr. Davies, his wife and child, lived with his parents in Eleanor Place, Twerton. That Saturday evening the whole family had met Mrs. Davies' parents and gone for a drink at the Full Moon. At around 11.00 pm Eric Davies was standing at the foot of his garden, saying goodnight to his in-laws:

> I was at the top of the steps when I saw the first chandelier (string of flares) across the south-east slopes of the city, over Southdown. I said, 'Bath is for it.' I was asked why, and I said I had seen it before. I'd just prepared the coal-house as a shelter with some stools and a chair. We got our parents down from upstairs and just then the sirens went. We went to the coal-house but my father refused and he sat in the armchair by the fire, in the house itself.

The sirens sounded. Few people seemed to take any notice at first. The sirens always went when Bristol was being attacked. A few curious souls showed sufficient interest to look or go outside. Mr. Gittens, a merchant seaman on leave, lived in Marlborough Lane, which James Webster was patrolling, and was one of those who did venture out. After a few minutes he could see flares to the north of the city, in the direction of Sham Castle. Others were falling in the Kingsmead area. One woman recalls some of the first falling over nearby Green Park. Still, there was little concern. The sight of cascading incendiary bombs was nothing new. Stray dusters had landed in Bath before. Mr. Gittens, like Eric Davies, sensed these were not dropped in error, though; and Mr. Gittens, realising that incendiaries invariably presaged high-explosive bombs, swiftly took cover. He heard the whistle of one of the first of such bombs as it followed the incendiaries into Kingsmead.

Anne Marks, then a child of nine, lived there, in New King Street to be precise. Her family had heard the siren and chose to ignore it:

Bath had had no real raids up until then ... so when one siren sounded on the Saturday night of April 25th, my mum and I had grown blasé and stayed in bed, thinking the raiders would pass over as usual. Strange, though, the gunfire and bombs sounded very close for Bristol. Our house at that time was composed of flats and the elderly lady upstairs came down to our flat. Apparently she had seen from her window some incendiary bombs dropped quite close and was frightened. Mum decided that we should get up – my dad was already on fire-watching duty. As we passed downstairs, one landing window shattered in our faces and for the first time I really felt scared.

A string of three high-explosive bombs had landed. Two fell in nearby Kingsmead Street, causing substantial damage. The third fell 100 yards further west, in New King Street. It was this bomb that had shattered the window. It burst in the road, digging a large crater and totally demolishing two of the large Georgian houses nearby. Number 7 New King Street collapsed in upon itself killing eleven inhabitants. This included seven members of one family alone, the Fords. Mrs. Ford and her six children died; Mr. Ford was elsewhere, serving in the army. Casualties in other houses nearby brought the death toll from this one bomb to twenty. Perhaps, like many, these people had paid little attention to the sirens. The high-explosives that awoke others to the real danger had merely caught those at 7 New King Street where they stood. Without the protection of a shelter, they never stood a chance as their house collapsed around them.

Kingsmead was to suffer some of the worst bombing of all. Assorted experts had long feared that the poorly constructed Georgian houses of Bath might collapse like packs of cards if they were bombed. In fact, some people in Kingsmead owed their lives to the fact that such houses had roomy and substantial cellars extending well under the road. They made good shelters. Betty Tutt of Kingsmead Square spent the night in the cellar with the occupants of all three flats above. Elizabeth Harden, nearby, sheltered in her basement although it also doubled as a store for her grocery business. Anne Marks also took cover:

> The people in the bottom flat asked us to join them. They had visitors from London who had survived the London bombings of 1940 and they were able to reassure us a bit. I found myself half under a camp bed huddled in a blanket. There was a candle lit in the room and as bombs dropped, the foundations of the house shook and the candle flame flickered. I can remember being mesmerised by it. I had every confidence that we would survive and looked forward to the morning when I could go out and survey the damage.

The actual sound of bombs falling finally galvanised most people into action. In the modern houses on the outskirts of the city, the majority of people sheltered in the Morrison table shelter. Others went under the stairs. Jill Clayton was a child of eight. She woke up half way down the stairs under her mother's arm:

> We went into the front, best room and my father turned the sofa against the wall so that the seat was down and the back horizontal. He pushed me under this and simultaneously there was a tremendous bang and the windows were blown in. I learnt later it was a shelter in an opposite garden that had a direct hit. There were two girls there I remember, billetees of about twenty, who taught me in Sunday school and they were killed.

Those who had an Anderson shelter in the garden faced a daunting sprint to safety. One woman remembers her family racing for the shelter while bullets flew overhead. Some ignored official advice to stay put. One mother in Kingsmead Street sent her two young children out of the house to seek a public shelter. They never got there. Next morning their bodies were found in the street. Their faces were studded with broken glass. Some, however, were actually escorted from their homes to nearby public shelters:

> I was aged eight and lived with my mother and grandmother who was deaf and blind. The sirens went and we got up. Then the Air Raid Warden, Mr. Horwood, came and knocked on our door. He said 'Come along Mrs. Heskins. Everyone's in the shelter but you. Hurry up!' My grandmother was a little slow and we later discovered that we were the last to evacuate that stretch of houses. As we came out of the front door another warden, Mr. Howell, took my hand and led me across Mount Road towards the shelter at Twerton Roundhill. We walked slightly ahead. Another two wardens were hurrying along my mother and grandmother but grandmother wouldn't be hurried. We were only partly dressed and my underwear wasn't properly buttoned.

SATURDAY NIGHT: THE FIRST RAID

It was like daylight outside. The sky seemed alight. It would suddenly light up with bright sheets of light. You could see the aircraft come over. They were machine-gunning as they came over Twerton Roundhill. You could see the red tracer bullets flying. I looked up and saw a 'plane machine-gunning along the back of the allotments. It seemed to confront us. The aircraft was glass-fronted and a face was visible. It was really pale in the light. They followed one behind the other, every half a minute or so. They seemed to skim the top of the Roundhill and then drop down towards the city centre.

(Faith Dolman)

Others had more immediate problems. James Webster the fire-watcher had heard the sirens and believed it was a raid on Bristol. This view was reinforced by the fact that he saw the searchlights in action there. Then he heard a bomb drop in the direction of his home in Crescent Gardens, a few hundred yards away. Rushing to the scene, he found that the bomb had torn a deep hole in the road. It had ignited the gas main which continued to burn throughout the night. A bicycle shop opposite, containing a large supply of paraffin, had gone up like a flaming torch: and there were about a dozen incendiary bombs burning on the roof of his house. The fire-watcher was having to extinguish the fires on his own property. James Webster climbed onto the roof. With the aid of a shovel, he began to scoop up the bombs and throw them onto the road below.

The Fire Service was already in action. One of its first active squads became involved in a moment of black comedy. As the incendiary bombs fell, the Fire Chiefs assumed it was a raid on Bristol. A squad was detached to go and help there. Almost immediately, the firemen involved realised that Bath was more than an accidental target. The heavy bombs were already falling before they left the city centre. It was soon so bad, that in order to avoid cratered roads, they had to make a detour through Victoria Park. One fireman had the misfortune to drive past his own house and see it in flames. However, orders were orders and it was not until the squad reported in Bristol that they were allowed to return and tackle the fires in Bath.

The other Civil Defence services were also in action. They suffered an immediate handicap. One of the first bombs along the Upper Bristol Road, perhaps that which fell outside James Webster's house, severed the telephone links between Apsley House and the centre of the city. Major Pickard, the overall commander at the headquarters, called out the despatch riders and messenger boys. They provided an excellent service, but one that obviously could not compete with a fully working telephone system. With communications crippled, some personnel reported to the central police station instead. Most went to Apsley House, as intended. Once they arrived, they often found there was little they could do. Dr. Bernard Astley-Weston, who was then head of the casualty service, remembers that much of the careful planning went by the board as there was only time for urgent necessities. The telephonists had no time to write messages in triplicate. The various heads just sent out the equipment that they thought was necessary. The personnel at Apsley House, to some extent, had just to sit back and allow the crews to act on their own initiative. In theory the ambulances, for example, would complete a task and then report back to their depot. This would telephone Apsley House to notify them of the ambulance's availability. In practice, damaged communications weakened the system and many ambulances found so many other cases to deal with that they had no time to report back. Dr. Astley-Weston found that once the few crews that could be contacted were out, he just had to wait until some became available again.

The wardens and police were soon out. Sidney Coleman, as head warden of the Holloway area, was moving around, conducting people to shelters and trying to calm down the more agitated. Often, this meant having to leave one's own family to fend for itself. His wife, Emily Coleman, spent the night in the cupboard under the stairs, only to hear one of the windows fly across the room as a result of a near miss. Mr. Hayward, a special constable, took his wife around to his sister and then went on duty in the Moorland Road area. There was a rumour of some panic there, at the Scala public shelter.

The services were also dealing with the other major problem at the start of the raids, Frank Selwyn, who was working with a rescue team, spent his time ushering people into a shelter in the Newbridge area of Weston, dealing swiftly with one potential tragedy:

As the sirens went, I went out to see that all the sick were sheltered. It was quite dark, but as I went out someone said, 'Put that bloody light out,' despite the fact that an incendiary had fallen on a little girl's bed in a house nearby. It singed and destroyed her teddy, about which she was crying, and had fallen into the corner of the room. We attacked the incendiary with a jet of water from the stirrup-pump and put it out quickly so that it only blistered the paintwork.

Fire could spread rapidly ... so could fear:

I went along to the gasworks. I found practically the whole of Hungerford Road on fire. The Germans had dropped fire bombs on the way to the gasworks, perhaps. All the houses were burning, being made from coal dust, I suppose. In Hungerford Road many of the owners panicked and ran, rather than fight the fire. If they had stayed they could probably have put them out easily. I stopped some people from going but some men just left the keys to their houses with me. Two young men just dashed off.

Incendiary bombs were far less dangerous than high-explosive ones. If the former were attacked promptly they could be extinguished easily. Individual householders were expected to deal with their own bombs. Unoccupied buildings had to have their own fire-watchers by law. If people did panic then a small fire could become a danger. The only other fear was that there would be such a concentration of incendiaries in an area that it could overwhelm the dousers. When the defenders stood firm, they could usually cope:

> I went out and found a house which the occupants had left, and left us with the key. I saw we therefore had to keep the fires down. We did extremely well in the Newbridge Hill area while servicemen on leave helped to fight fires in Chelsea Road. I had a good sports coat on and ruined it. I also got a bomb out of the rafters of one house, and helped to empty it of furniture.
>
> (Frank Selwyn)

With the best will in the world, not all could be saved. Mr. Webster was still grappling with the bombs that were trying to burn their way through his roof. He managed to throw all off but one:

> There was no water. The last incendiary had already caught the beams on fire, and I couldn't do a thing. Directly they hit, they went up in flames. I soon realised the last one was too much. I was on the roof taking tiles off so that I could try to saw through and remove the beams. However, I was removed as Jerry was machine-gunning ... the last one burnt the roof, and the back bedroom fell in.

The machine-gunning was rarely fatal – but naturally disconcerting. The fear of being seen by a bomber led to some trying to present as small a target as possible. Sidney Coleman was one of many who felt particularly vulnerable with his special leader's white helmet. He threw it off as he lay down in Holloway, as a stream of bullets scythed down the road. Frank Selwyn had rather a different problem. While fire-fighting in Chelsea Road, he realised his helmet appeared too small. In fact, it was his wife's, who was also in Civil Defence. She was a first aider at the Homestead post. She found her husband in Chelsea Road, swapped helmets, and then both dived for cover as another aircraft dived down and machine-gunned the area. It was not only the machine-guns, but the bombs themselves that kept people's heads down. Mr. Jackson, the 'veteran' of the Dolemeads bombing, put it succinctly:

> There were so many bombs, it was suicide to do anything. You just had to lie down until everything was clear. There was no use creating more casualties.

It was essential that some people were out at all times though. Leslie Nott was one of the despatch riders. Early in the raid he had joined up with another rider, Wally Angus. The two were driving along Winchester Road in Oldfield Park, with Mr. Angus leading. A bomb landed in the road ahead. Disorientated by the blast, Leslie Nott shot down the road and took cover in the Scala shelter. Mr. Angus was nowhere to be seen.

There was no point in adding needlessly to the casualties. Grace Selwyn's superior at the Homestead was Mrs. Marjorie Horsell, and through no fault of her own, she was finding it very difficult to get to her post. In some ways it was a matter of very bad timing. Every weekday Mrs. Horsell slept at the Homestead. At the weekend she stayed at home in a house just off Bear Flat. If the sirens went, she would be picked up. That Saturday the sirens had sounded and she had waited for transport. None had come and, in a temporary lull, she had gone to the Bear Garage. Eventually, she managed to get a car to the post at St. James's Parade.

That depot was, however, already out of action. Robert Smith, a superintendent there, had been out on an exercise when the sirens went. He had quickly returned to his depot. As he stood in a downstairs room, there was a crash in the room above. Mr. Smith ran upstairs to find the blackouts down. He looked around for a blanket to put up instead. Then he noticed that on one of the two camp beds in the room sat an unexploded bomb. It had come diagonally through the ceiling, slightly injuring a messenger boy there in the accompanying fall of debris. Mr. Smith evacuated the depot but, for a while, messages were still coming in by the telephone. Mrs. Woolmer, an expectant mother, continued to man it until there was no more need. She later received a reward; well deserved, as the telephone happened to be in the same room as the bomb.

Meanwhile, Grace Selwyn had reached her destination, the Homestead. The first casualties were already coming in. Yet there was a sense of anti-climax. Certainly, it was an initial shock as the grimy and dirty injured began to arrive, but a number of the first aiders expected to have to deal with far more casualties than were trickling in at present. The ambulances were out, and picking up casualties. Don Tuddenham was sent to Locksbrook Road to pick up the injured, but found none. Instead, he suffered a machine-gun attack that sent him diving for cover. His next job was at Marlborough Lane where he was told there were two dead; but at this stage there was no point in dealing with any but the injured, and he had to leave them. James Webster remembers seeing dead there:

> I found one chap in Marlborough Lane, he was split open like a kipper. A blast had got him. Earlier I had seen him drunk and shouting.

There were relatively few casualties as yet. The bulk of this first raid was made up of incendiary bombs. These were effective at burning houses and creating an obvious target for succeeding waves of aircraft. Luckily, they were poor anti-personnel weapons. The high-explosive bombs were much larger and deadlier to human life. One line of such bombs stitched its way across Henrietta Park, digging a number of holes and filling the trees with shrapnel, but otherwise causing little damage. Another bomb landed on the recreation ground, severely warping a stand. It also caused some worry to a nearby policeman, Fred Self, who saw a series of sheets of corrugated iron shoot up into the sky and come down like scythes.

These were the main heavy bombs in the centre of the

city. The chief load in this first raid fell through Kingsmead, destroying the front of the 16th century Abbey Church House on the way; wreaking havoc in the goods yard of the Midland Railway, and disturbing a number of graves in St. James' graveyard. Only the west of the city suffered a more concentrated attack. Another of the first heavy bombs had opened up a gas and water main at the bottom of Brook Road, near the gasworks. The blast had been sufficient to move a shelter in the road some three inches, without injury to any of the occupants. The burning gas jet was immediately noticeable though, and must have drawn further attention to the area. Soon after, the first bombs landed on the gasworks themselves: not surprising when one remembers that the well-lit area was also clearly marked on the Germans' aerial maps. The first landed in a coal dump. Fragments punched a number of holes in Number 5 Gasholder. The second caused more damage. It made a direct hit on Number 4 holder and blew in the sides of Number 3 which in turn collapsed and burst into flames. A third bomb wreaked havoc amongst various works buildings. Two motorbike despatch riders inadvertently discovered the damage; as they drove over the bridge nearby, they found themselves in leaking creosote, hot and a foot deep.

Within a short time there were a number of fires in and around the gasworks. Units of the fire service were sent out:

I went first to a fire in Chancellors Yard, in Lower Bristol Road. Chancellor House had been hit. There were people in a Morrison table shelter there, and the bomb had set a gas supply pipe on fire inside the house. I bent the pipe and turned the flame away. It wasn't our business to get people out so we telephoned for the rescue people.

I was sent then to the petrol depot opposite Pitmans which was said to be on fire. But there was no fire there. I reported to the Modern Motors sub-station. The appliances were out at a fire in Bellots Road at Parsons & Vezey, the haulage contractor. There was nothing else to do so we went there, where we were under the command of a brigade company officer. We were dousing a recently arrived pile of tyres. There were bursts from the German planes along Bellots Road. They sieved Mr. Parsons' own car in his garage, and the garage door. We dived down but we still had to keep hold of the hose.

We got water from the static tank outside Twerton cemetery gate. We used all the water there and only then did we go to the river at the bottom of Roseberry Road to refill the static tank. We put the fire out but all the time the gas main at the bottom of Brook Road was on fire. The main was twisted up and there was a flame coming from it so the area was still lit up. We didn't dare put the fire out lest it gassed people, and we couldn't turn it off.

(Tom Gale, Leading Fireman)

In some ways, the worst off were those in the shelters. They could hear only the occasional bomb and had no real idea what was going on outside. In intermittent gaps during the bombing, some people would look outside. Often this gave the wrong impression, as a quick glance at a few major fires convinced some that this first raid was more destructive than it actually was. When the all-clear finally sounded at around 1.20 am, there was some opportunity to discover what had been happening. Anne Marks' father returned from digging people out in Lower Bristol Road, a gash across his forehead. Like many others, Eric Davies left his shelter and walked to the bottom of the garden:

I left the shelter and went to look. The gasworks were already burning. That was the biggest conflagration but there were fires everywhere.

Thus, the city was, in part, well ablaze and an easy target for a second attack.

CHAPTER SIX

Saturday: Raid Two

For many people, the two raids on that first night merge practically into one continuous experience, with only a brief gap in between. In fact, the official records reveal a good three-hour interval. It is obviously difficult to recall exact times some forty years after the event. It has also been noted, in other raids, that in moments of stress one can easily become disorientated. There are other reasons. In particular, the sporadic nature of the first raid had not produced a concentrated attack; at times there had been many aircraft over the city. Sometimes there had been none. Silence did not necessarily mean the end of the raid, merely a temporary lull at times. It was also extremely late when the first raid ended and, as some have said, they were so tired by then that they noticed very little.

Faith Dolman, who had run to the shelter at Twerton Roundhill, spent the whole night there. Candles provided a few pinpoints of light. There was a little singing at times. Faith's grandmother prayed out loud. Her mother, in some agitation, talked a great deal. Most dozed, fitfully. The wardens made periodic excursions outside but few bothered to leave after the first all-clear and most did not leave until it was almost dawn. A large number of people, having taken shelter, were loath to move until daylight, when they could know for certain that the bombers were not returning.

Some went outside. A few believed the Germans had finished for the night. Others just wanted to see what was happening while there was a lull in the proceedings. At the Scala shelter one family and their friends went home for a quick cup of tea. When they went back, they had to sit at the opposite end of the shelter to the one they were at before. At Stanley Road the Pooles' whist evening had been rudely interrupted. The couple had stayed with their in-laws during the first raid. Then the mother-in-law decided that she wanted to go to the public shelter at the end of the road. The rest agreed. In Kingsmead, a number left their shelters. Betty Tutt emerged from her cellar in Kingsmead Square and found that everything seemed grey with dust. Further along, in New King Street, Anne Marks was also up. Her mother was asked by the elderly neighbour upstairs to accompany her to relatives in Rivers Street to check they were safe. Luckily, Mrs. Marks' mother feared another raid and declined to do so.

In Oldfield Park Doreen Wall, then single, lived with her parents. During the lull her brother came down from Beechen Cliff to see them. He wanted to stay, but his mother sent him back to his home. A number of people were returning home after being forced to take shelter earlier in the evening. Two men walked from the centre of the city. They parted at Roseberry Road as one lived there. The other walked on to Twerton. Another man, a Mr. Wilcox, also lived in Roseberry Road. He kept pigs in the direction of Englishcombe, and during the lull went to see if they were alright. As he left home he passed a dead body, laid out under the railway arch nearby.

Some had work to do at home. Hubert Jackson, no relation to the policeman, spent the quiet hours cleaning up plaster in his house at Ivy Grove, Southdown, after the ceiling fell in as a result of a near miss. As yet, few people had to cope with major problems. A fair number of bombs had been dropped. Some fires, in particular at the gasworks, were still burning. But even some of the Civil Defence personnel found they had time to go home as there was little for them to do. Fred Short, who had escorted people to the shelter in Roseberry Road, went home to Odd Down to check that his family was safe. Dr. Mary Middlemas, who was working at the Snow Hill First Aid Post, returned temporarily to her nearby home in the Paragon. Henry Hamlin stayed at his Rescue Party Post. He was still wondering where his immediate superior was, because he had not arrived at the depot. This senior colleague was the previously mentioned Wally Angus, and as yet no one knew he was a casualty. In the lull, it was possible to get the more badly injured to hospital. At St. Martin's Dr. Frederick Kohn, a veteran of the London bombing, had long ago set aside an empty ward in case there was an attack on Bath. This acted as a receiving ward. Any casualties would be taken there and looked at by Dr. Kohn or one of his three housemen. They would decide which should have first priority for treatment. The lull gave him time to sort out those who were seriously injured and those who needed immediate operations. Only the worst casualties went to the hospitals though, the lighter injuries going to the first aid posts. There were also a number of people whose houses were in some way or another uninhabitable and who just needed shelter and some comfort after distressing experiences. These people were directed to the rest centres. At one, the Salvation Army hostel near Bath Spa railway station, was Muriel Gough:

We lived in the centre of Bath, in Kingston Road. After the first all-clear, my seventeen year old brother went off on his bike as a messenger. I went to the Salvation Army hostel about 100 yards away to help. Our warden, Mr. Angel, was directing groups in from different districts. One group came from Cheltenham Street. Some had only slight injuries. An unexploded bomb had dropped near the Electric Light Works. It had raised the paving stone up. Mr. Angel had been walking along when he tripped up. He caught his chin either on the fin of the bomb or on a paving stone. He came along. The Salvation Army women were there. We asked if we could help. We got out cups and saucers. They brought in a bunch of lads. There was a boys' remand home in Kingsmead. A warden was in charge of them. Incendiary bombs had set the home alight.

A mobile canteen came from Bristol. There was no hot water available. The man in charge asked for some. I said I'd go home for some. I'd just got back to the hostel when the siren went again.

The other major service still in action was the Fire Brigade. Tom Gale, having helped to extinguish the fire in Bellots Road, was still refilling the static tank that he had had to drain:

We were still clearing up after putting out the fire at the

haulage contractors. We heard the siren for the second raid. I heard a bomb and flung myself under the wall. I was already down, supporting my chest off the ground, when the bomb dropped. It was a 1,000 pounder in Roseberry Road. The blast knocked me out. I felt like I was being torn apart inside. There was debris, muck and stone on top of me. A policeman patted me on either side of my face. He was calling 'Come on! It's all on fire!' The booster at the top of Bellots Road had fallen on top of the pump and was no use. The two at the static tank were okay as they'd taken cover. But I was worried about the rest of the crew, especially those near the river. I went there, but it was okay. They'd heard the bomb and dived under the pump. The blast had taken its bonnet off. The hose was flattened and there was a lump of red brick on the engine. We had no appliances and no 'phones. The flight works were on fire. I sent a man to the Fire Station to get ten pumps but heard nothing. The Fire Force Commander sent a Boy Scout who did get through, with a request for 20 pumps.

At Roseberry Road there was no fire. It was all blasted down. The bomb had pitched on the surface shelters – the people were gone. It had also broken the main sewer and the crater had filled in as deep as the river. I saw no survivors, none at all.

No doubt the bomb had been intended for the gasworks. It fell short by a few hundred yards. It landed almost directly on top of the brick built shelter to which Fred Short had earlier directed a number of people. Seven of the terraced houses nearby were instantly demolished. The dead numbered at least thirty and were mostly the very young and the very old; they were predominantly female. At Number 17, for example, one of those completely flattened, four members of the Smith family died, mother and three daughters. The youngest was only sixteen months old. Only the husband survived. Number 13 did not collapse at once but much of the interior was destroyed. A Miss Goddard was crushed by the debris. Her body was not to be found for another three weeks. The man who had walked from the city centre in the lull was killed. Mr. Wilcox, visiting his pigs, survived. His wife, who remained at home, did not. From some houses, a number of injured were removed. John O'Shea, a young man, was recovered from Number 20. He was taken away to hospital.

The Poole family, parents, son and daughter-in-law, were standing near another brick-built street shelter, this time in Stanley Road. The parents were already inside when the second raid began. But it seems there had been a change of plan by at least one of the company. Alma Poole, the daughter-in-law, suddenly changed her mind and decided she wanted to go back to her home in Second Avenue. Perhaps she had already just left the shelter. Her husband Sydney was standing in the entrance. They must have heard, close by, a series of explosions. One aircraft dropped a line of high-explosive bombs. The first landed 150 yards away, across the railway. It hit another row of terraces, Victoria Road. A delayed action bomb, it was assumed to have detonated only after it had penetrated the roof of house Number 3. An explosion at such a low level was particularly devastating. Twenty-one houses were destroyed, yet casualties were surprisingly low, with only about eight dead. Many must have taken cover in the brick street shelters. Even these suffered some damage. One had a series of small holes punched in its roof, although none of the inhabitants was hurt.

A second and third bomb landed either side of the railway line itself, near the Brougham Hayes bridge. There was slight damage to the line but no casualties. The fourth bomb came down on top of Stanley Road. The fifth landed on the street shelter there. Amongst the casualties were the Poole family. Neighbours rushed to help pull the injured from the wreckage of the shelter. Both parents were found still alive and were taken to hospital. A Mr. Padfield dragged two women out. One was already dead. The other was alive, but died as she was laid down on the ground nearby. It was assumed later that one of these was Alma Poole, the daughter-in-law. At the time, no one was in a position to take any notice, least of all her husband. The blast had robbed him of all sense of hearing and he was taken to hospital suffering from severe shock. All that was ever found were a few pieces of Mrs. Poole's coat amongst the debris nearby, to prove that she died there.

Perhaps the greatest tragedy was that if the family had stayed at the parents' home or even gone to the son's, they would all undoubtedly have survived. Neither home was severely damaged by the bombing. The street shelters had come under serious attack at the start of this second raid, and as expected had been unable to stand up to a direct hit. The concentration of people there had led to correspondingly high casualties. On the other hand, a similar shelter in Victoria Road had no doubt saved many lives. However, the bomb here had not fallen on the shelter itself. In this series of shelter direct hits in the early part of the raid, there was one more to come.

The Scala shelter was of a more substantial type than the ordinary street ones. It was a semi-sunk tubular steel shelter, surrounded by earth and sand bags. Leslie Nott, the despatch rider, had decided it was time to leave. By then there were at least twenty people in the shelter:

There were people with coats there, others with pyjamas. I laughed and joked with them. There were two girls there and one lady in a fur coat. They were saying 'Come on, let's have a dance,' presumably to keep their spirits up. One even had a mouth organ.

Perhaps the high spirits were the result of a certain degree of fear. There were a number of special constables, part time police, in the shelter as well. They were obviously taking cover but possibly calming people at the same time. One was Mr. Barrow, a teacher at West Twerton School. Another was Mr. Parsons, an invalid who had been unable to join the army; this was his first day as a special constable. There was also a Mr. Hayward. It was he who had brought his wife to his sister's home, for safety, at the start of the first raid:

I had to go. I got about 100 yards to Hunt's the Undertakers. I saw tracer bullets and was pulled to the side of the road by a policeman. We both jumped into the gutter. Then the bomb fell on the shelter.

(Leslie Nott)

To be precise, the bomb had fallen on one end of the shelter. Some of those at the opposite end did survive, they included the family that had moved places after going home for a cup of tea during the lull. Most died, however. The eight special constables were killed. Mr. Parsons' first day was also his last. Their commander, a Mr. Packwood, was crushed by falling masonry. At least six more people died, apart from the constables. The blast was so great that one man was blown straight out of the shelter. His body was found in the road sometime later. It is impossible to give exact figures of those killed. Sometimes the death certificates record only the dead person's home address, and not the place of death. At the Scala the sheer force of the blast was magnified by being concentrated in such a small place. Some bodies were blown and squeezed into the gaps between the outside wall of the shelter and the inner row of sandbags. Some were rendered unidentifiable. On one form from the Scala shelter, the body is listed unidentified: but the heading 'Male/Female' has been crossed out and above is written 'indistinguishable'. Others were literally blown to pieces. Apart from the special constables, most of the dead came from Third Avenue. Once again, if they had stayed at home, they would probably have survived. None of their houses suffered any greater damage than loss of windows and roof tiles.

Yet Third Avenue was hit by at least one bomb and at least one man who stayed home there was killed. The Oldfield Park area was hit by so many bombs on this first night that home or shelter made little difference. Moorland Road, the main shopping area in Oldfield Park, suffered a series of explosions. The Livingstone public house went up in flames. A street warden, Sam Hayward, no relation to the one at the Scala, who lived nearby, could hear bottles exploding there because of the heat. King Edward Road, yet another terraced row, took at least one direct hit. The newly completed church of St. Bartholomew's was severely damaged as well. Along Lower Oldfield Park so many of the large Victorian houses were destroyed that the road was blocked by rubble for hundreds of yards. At one end of the road, the cul-de-sac of Thornbank Place was hit by two further bombs. Nearby, Cheltenham Street was largely wrecked by another series of explosions.

Further west, Twerton was hit just as badly. The railway embankment took two hits. A number of bombs fell further up the hill. One landed in Eleanor Place:

The sirens went again. We had just got downstairs and were just in the shelter, except for father, when there was a bang. I heard two or three bombs. Two landed in the field behind us. The second was louder. I didn't hear the third which hit us. My mother was blown so that her head was pushed between my legs. There was a stone on her back as the stones had come through the stairs and pushed her forward. The stairs and door held my head. I couldn't even scratch. I could just feel my wife's shoulder. She was to the left with the baby on her knee. I couldn't remember anything for a few minutes because of concussion. There was blood which was probably from my nose. I couldn't do anything. For a few seconds I tried to get out but it just brought more debris down. We were all afraid to speak in case there was no answer. My wife spoke first, then I did. It was hard as we were covered with plaster, dirt and debris from head to toe.

Luckily, most of the debris had blown across, and not on top of us, and onto the front. There was debris all over the front garden. That part of the house above ground level was down. All the front of the bottom part of the house was down as well, except for the inside retaining wall. The stairs were below the retaining wall and they were the only thing left. They were firmly embedded in the wall. So was a shelf held on by big L-brackets with a heavy box of tools, all of which was above my wife's head. We were between the stairs and the wall and all the rest was on top of us. For the next hour we could hear aircraft going up and down the valley. There was much noise ... I smelt burning. I didn't know everything had blown in on top. We could hear machine-gun bullets. At least we felt safe and there were very few bombs dropped after, but it shook above us sometimes.

(Eric Davies)

Other houses were destroyed as well. Doreen Wall had received a visit from her brother during the lull. Early in the second raid a bomb demolished the house next to hers, leaving Mrs. Wall and her parents trapped under the stairs. Florence Delve, who lived on Primrose Hill, stayed with her husband and two year old girl on a mattress under the dining table. She actually heard the bomb come whistling down. She was also one of the few who could accurately time the explosion: 4.45 am, the time when her clock stopped. The bomb landed in front of the house and tore up a line of seven or eight gardens. Mrs. Delve suffered temporary concussion. When she came to, the whole house had caved in; but there was only one storey above and the dining table could take the strain.

Hubert Jackson had spent the lull clearing up some fallen plaster. Along with his wife and son, he then took cover in their newly acquired Morrison table shelter. The netting at one end was left up, though, as Mrs. Jackson feared being trapped:

We didn't hear it. The bomb fell in soft earth. It uprooted everything and left a crater 30 feet in diameter and 15 feet deep. It took seven-eighths of the house; it uprooted it. It cracked the electric cable, and threw it up over the top of the house and it ended up pointing at my Home Guard jacket. The partition wall fell into our room and pushed my feet up; the shelter being open. I was lying on my son to protect him ... we were literally trapped, covered up. We didn't realise our predicament. Probably numbed by the explosion, we didn't hear the crash and didn't realise the house had come down. Where we were, we faced the back window and the corner that was still standing, but that was all, and it gave us the impression that there was only a little damage.

In a number of cases, once consciousness had returned and it was realised that all had survived, there was a certain amount of relief. The rescue services were bound to find them. It was also felt that having been hit once, there could be no further bombs on that site. There were other dangers. Hubert Jackson, while trapped, saw an incendiary bomb land just outside the window. Luckily it burnt itself out, while providing them with a little light. The greatest worry was that most houses still had open, coal fires. It was lucky that the raids were so late that most grates had cooled. However, some still had warmth, and if the house collapsed, then the glowing coals could easily start a blaze. Eric Davies and most of his family had taken cover. His father had refused to move from the front room, sitting in front of the fire's dying embers. Unable to move from the collapsed shelter, Mr. Davies had no idea what had happened to him.

Only one other area suffered a more concentrated attack. Once again, Kingsmead seemed marked out for particular attention. The word 'Bath' on the original German photo-map happens to be inscribed across Kingsmead. Perhaps it was the main aiming point. It certainly seemed so to the local inhabitants. Both Anne Marks and Betty Tutt took cover again. Ron Taylor spent the night with his father on the roof of their home at the corner of New King Street. Sparks and cinders landed continually on the roof and had to be thrown off: a good example of fire-watching in action. Even so, the Taylors were continually hampered by the German efforts. The bombers could be seen clearly and at times the machine-gunning was so close that both father and son had to take cover. They could see members of the Civil Defence services in the street below also having to lie down as the Germans passed over. One of them was Albert Davis, a rescue party leader, who faced a problem already encountered:

> We were in New King Street when Jerry was machine-gunning. The chief warden told me to tell the men to shelter. The nearest was in Queen Square. I fell into the gutter and put some paper over my head to protect myself against the machine-gunning. It was stupid but I did have my white hat on, and white hats were a target.

Once more, the low-level machine-gunning was a serious nuisance. Kay Oliver had walked to Prior Park Road during the lull, but the bombers returned unexpectedly. A stream of bullets sent her diving for cover. She went up the road on her hands and knees and could see the bullet-holes in the road next day. According to official records, no one died from machine-gunning on this first night. However low they were, bombers flying fast, and at night, could never hope to spray bullets very accurately. The random attacks certainly discouraged people from moving about. Firemen had to abandon attempts to douse flames at times. Key personnel could not get through to their posts and depots. Others had to take cover. Muriel Gough, at the Salvation Army hostel, was ordered out of the kitchen and away from the crockery. Any object could cause havoc if thrown about by an explosion. She was told to lie down as the bombs fell again. Mr. Jackson, the policeman, was similarly hampered:

> I had fourteen casualties in one shelter – the nearest first aid post was a mile away. It would have been suicide to move them, and as I knew where a doctor lived, I went to get him. The roof of his car was smashed in but we eventually got his bag out of it. We stayed in the shelter and calmed them down until we could move out.

Another person caught in the open was Marjorie Horsell. She was still trying to get to the Homestead First Aid Post. So far, she had reached St. James's Parade. That post had already been rendered inoperable because of the unexploded bomb there:

The ambulance driver said that he could go no further because of the glass and the rubble on the road ... I said I would walk. However, the sirens went again and then the bombs fell. I walked to Crescent Gardens where there were two houses that were a mass of flame. I know it sounds wrong, but it was a wonderful sight. I just stopped and looked ... I went along Upper Bristol Road but was stopped by a police inspector who said the road and the gasworks were a sea of flames. I took cover. The German 'planes were so low that I could see them in the 'planes and could see the tracer bullets. It was awful to see the faces in the 'planes.

The ambulances were out again. Theirs was not an easy task. As has already been explained, the complete lack of radio communication meant that they rarely went back to their depot. Having dealt with one incident, they were frequently directed by wardens to another in the same area. They were so busy that they could only deal with those who were still alive. The dead had to be left, although it was sometimes very difficult to tell whether someone was dead or alive. The main difficulty was the actual business of driving. Many ambulance drivers could hear bombs dropping nearby. In the blackout, it was difficult to see craters in the road or even the occasional unexploded bomb. There was some light at times. Houses on fire, plus a large number of flares and incendiaries provided some illumination. They also drew the attention of further German bombers.

The drivers had to cope with these new perils as best they could. Vic Penny had to abandon one vehicle after driving it into a crater. Another ambulance driver tended to drive past unexploded bombs rather than make lengthy detours, in order to get casualties to the hospital quickly.

One of my first incidents was at King Edward Road/Junction Road where I picked up the body of Wally Angus, the superintendent of Rescue Services, and a known colleague of mine. I went to Maple Grove where I picked up the body of Mrs. Dando, the wife of the furniture dealer in Wood Street. Her husband was a telephonist at the Bear ambulance depot. She sheltered her child from an incendiary and died in the process. I went down the Lower Bristol Road to a position midway between the Green Tree and the Midland Bridge. Peacock, a messenger boy, was with me. He had a good initiation into bodies. We were just loading this corpse when Jerry decided to drop a bomb in the river. It threw a great deal of muck out: dead fish, bicycles, bedsteads, etc. We shot under the ambulance to take cover from the muck, rather than the bomb.

(William Smith, ambulance driver)

Marjorie Horsell had finally reached her objective, the Homestead First Aid Post. She was not the only one to have had difficulty in getting there. The post had a nominal staff of just over a dozen, but a couple had never turned up even for the training sessions. One had been off to look after her husband while he was ill. It was later discovered that both were killed by a bomb, while at home. Other staff had to cope with their own injuries, or had to take cover and were unable to reach the post. Mrs. Horsell now joined Grace Selwyn and the half dozen regulars who had managed to arrive. By this time the casualties were coming in thick and fast:

We were volunteers there and inexperienced. The casualties started coming in and we didn't know where to begin. They were covered in dust and grime. We had stretchers on the floor for them. My first case was an old lady. A few days before the raids I had been collecting for charity and this old lady had asked if I knew if her grandson, who was in the navy, was safe. My husband found that his ship had been sunk. Anyway, this lady was completely scalped. It was a horrible beginning.

(Grace Selwyn)

Marjorie Horsell remembers the same case:

One or two of the casualties died. One little old lady whom I was asked to see had a bruised forehead. I went to lift up her hair and her scalp came off like a wig. I got her to hospital but she died ... The casualties, by and large, were usually the less serious; fractured legs, firemen overcome by smoke, shrapnel wounds and grazings. A number were badly shocked and were given hot water bottles and covered with a blanket. Only occasionally was anyone hysterical. The worst casualties were sent straight to hospital.

Most major and minor casualties were caused by high-explosive bombs. Incendiaries could burn but they were small and light and very rarely did they cause death. Most people could avoid them. Only if one was trapped might they prove deadly. The high-explosive bomb, on the other hand, sent out a vast expansion of gases and had the effect of a tremendously strong gust of wind. In a confined space, such as an air raid shelter, the concentrated blast could tear a person apart. Others were found without a mark on them. They were killed by the blast hitting the weaker internal organs, the lungs in particular. Sydney Poole lived, but his eardrums were severely damaged. However, blast itself was not always deadly. The human body is soft and can absorb it in a way that a rigid wall cannot. Both Tom Gale and Leslie Nott were near large explosions but suffered little injury. Sometimes the gust of wind could play strange tricks. At least one woman was found alive but naked, her clothes torn from her by a near miss.

More people died or were injured because such a fierce gale could turn the most innocuous of items into sharp, deadly weapons. Bomb fragments, stone and, in particular, glass caused many casualties. Muriel Gough had to leave the hostel kitchen because of the potential danger from the crockery there. Blast also caused injuries in a more indirect way. As we have seen, many houses suffered severe internal damage even when a bomb landed nearby, rather than as a direct hit. Collapsed ceilings and shattered windows created more casualties: and every bomb threw up a great deal of dust that could infect the slightest of wounds. Bath stone, being particularly soft, created a large amount of dust, and threatened to choke a number of the badly injured.

If in doubt, casualties were taken to the hospitals:

> We had just finished the sorting out when the second wave came over. When the raid was in full swing the casualties streamed in. We admitted over 100 casualties that night and treated many minor ones. All the casualties came in by ambulance. We just had to cope. I decided the priority of cases. Minor injuries were treated on the spot by the nursing staff. Most were given a tetanus serum injection. We could see what we had to do immediately and what could be left until later. If someone had a fractured leg they would be put in a comfortable position and dealt with later. Laceration had to be dealt with immediately in case of infection. We also had a few crush injuries – people trapped in rubble who were in more danger than those with simple fractures, and they had to be dealt with straightaway. The major casualties were: single or multiple fractures of bones; severe lacerations and foreign bodies – metal and especially glass, a horrible thing. One chap had an ear wound with a piece of glass in his cheek as big as the palm of my hand.
>
> (Dr. Kohn)

The Salvation Army hostel also had people coming in. A number were slightly injured but most were merely seeking comfort. Within a short time the hostel was packed, and drinks were being handed out. Mrs. Gough found that there was a certain degree of shock, especially after people had trailed through the streets in the dark first. Some were crying. Quite naturally there were a fair number of shock cases. Bath had never been blitzed. Few of its citizens had ever experienced a serious air raid. The dislocation caused by the sight of sudden death and the destruction of well-known landmarks caused much distress. In the midst of such disorder, some people tried to cling to a known routine even when it was rather inappropriate. At the height of the raid, one young man was severely reprimanded for showing a light. Yet this was in Brook Road. The gasworks opposite were well ablaze. Roseberry Road had been flattened. Nearby, Elm Grove Terrace had been largely destroyed by two or three bombs. In Brook Road itself, the shelter had been damaged. A number of houses in the road were flattened. One light could hardly, in all honesty, draw down much more trouble to the area.

Children, in particular, found it difficult to comprehend this new experience. Jill Clayton, then aged eight, had already seen the windows of her house blown in as she sheltered behind the sofa:

> I learnt later it was a shelter in an opposite garden that had a direct hit. There were two girls there I remember, billetees of about twenty, who taught me in Sunday School and they were killed.
>
> For the rest of the night it was all noise and clamour. My father was one of the few middle-aged men around, so people kept coming to him, asking for advice. A young girl came in and sat in the corner. She was given a cup of tea and was immediately sick all over the carpet. I thought my mother would be furious. She wasn't, of course. My mother said that a baby had been brought in but no one knew whose it was. I wasn't allowed to see it as it was badly injured. A doctor came in later and my mother was very upset because he said the baby was dead.

Panic never became widespread, partly because very few

people were having to face the full horrors of a bombing onslaught. Despite the heavy losses in particular cases, the bulk of the city's population spent the night under cover, hearing the occasional bomb burst, and with little knowledge of what was going on. The injured were a relatively small proportion of the populace. Many of these showed no sign of panic. Indeed, one sign of shock can be a passive acceptance of whatever is happening, rather than hysteria. Few homes were as busy as the Claytons'. One thing that struck those of the Civil Defence forces that had to be out during the raids was the absence of any other people around. At individual incidents there would be wardens, firemen, the injured and dazed survivors. Elsewhere there was no one to be seen.

The bombing was heavy but rarely concentrated. Kingsmead was extensively hit. Oldfield Park suffered a series of heavy blows. In other areas there were incidents but only of an isolated nature. Southdown and north Bath, for example, received a number of single bombs. These could still cause heavy casualties. One bomb dropped just off Southgate Street, in Howells Court, and killed at least sixteen people. It wiped out the Rattray family – mother, father and seven children. The Civil Defence services stood up well to this challenge. Communications may have been in pieces. Areas lacked facilities at times. Machine-gunning disrupted aid. However, there was never any real lack of assistance. From early on they had been reinforced by outside help, much of it with experience elsewhere.

Despatch riders were sent to the outskirts of the city to escort rescue teams new to the area. One first aid post had a visit from one motorcyclist, later on, who had driven all the way from Coventry, through the night, with the offer of assistance. There was never a lack of help. One woman remembers seeing a continuous stream of ambulances on the way to the Royal United Hospital, even when the raids were still going on.

Apsley House continued to organise Civil Defence as best it could. Soon there was a great deal of overcrowding. Outside assistance made for the control centre. Senior personnel went there. Bombed out Civil Defence depots, such as St. James's Parade, tended to relocate to Apsley House as well. By the end of the night the road nearby was crowded with parked vehicles. Many had their sidelights still burning. They were clearly visible from the air:

> There was a line of cars by the house. They could be seen in the moonlight. A German with a single bomb dived down onto the house. All but six of those there went down to the cellars. It was packed. The aircraft flew over four or five times. It released the bomb. It hit the tower of Apsley House, ricocheted, bounced onto the lawn and exploded. The tower was split but of the personnel only one had an ear nicked and one was cut above the kneecap. That was the end of the raid.
>
> (Don Tuddenham)

The house also lost most of its windows. One window frame shot across the room. A mass of brickwork squashed Dr. Astley-Weston's car, flat. The bomb also destroyed most of the records collected from the previous raid: but it does seem to have been one of the last bombs dropped before dawn appeared and the last of the bombers flew off.

CHAPTER SEVEN

Sunday

In the early morning of 26th April, the British and German High Commands took stock of the previous night's raids. The third successive raid by Bomber Command on Rostock had been the best so far. Goebbels noted his disappointment. Hitler was furious and blamed the anti-aircraft batteries at the city for failing adequately to deter the enemy. On the other hand, there was the attack on Bath. German radio announced details of the raid. The report spoke in general terms of a massed attack on Bath with thousands of explosive and incendiary bombs. Large fires were said to be visible from a distance, particularly in the centre of the city. The attack, it was announced, was an act of revenge for the bombing of 'cultural monuments' in old German towns. Great stress was laid on the revenge aspect of the raid. The fact that old German towns were being avenged by attacking an old British town was not emphasised.

In Britain, the appropriate Ministry, that of Home Security, began cautiously. It first reported enemy activity over the south-west of England. In one city, casualties and damage were 'rather heavy'. Bath was not mentioned by name. This had been common practice earlier in the war. The stray bombs that had fallen in 1941 had been written off in the press, but to prevent the Germans realising where they had hit, Bath was not mentioned by name. This raid was rather different. It soon became apparent that the bombers had planned to hit the city and there was no use in keeping the name a secret. Also, it was soon realised that Bath was such a well-known city that to publicise its destruction could only be good in the sense that it would put the Germans in an even worse light. However, details were still kept vague, lest the Germans pinpoint where their bombs fell. The *Daily Telegraph* reported that a grandstand had been badly damaged; the one that had flown across the sky in front of Mr. Fred Self. A few Georgian houses were destroyed. There were several casualties in a public shelter opposite a cinema. The Scala cinema was not mentioned by name. The newspapers had mixed views. They were indignant that the Georgian city of Bath had been attacked; yet they also reported with some accuracy that it was the more modern areas of the city that had sustained the most damage. It was the Victorian 'working class areas' that had taken the brunt of the attack. Most greatly underestimated the extent of the destruction. It was said that two families had been killed by a bomb in a working class area. Far heavier casualties had been caused by single bombs.

The papers laid greater stress on another aspect of the attack; and, for quite different reasons, so had the Germans. The German radio broadcast had commented on intense opposition by British night-fighters to create the vision of an heroic Luftwaffe, battling its way through to its target; and, presumably, towards a military target if there were so many squadrons defending it. The British newspapers took the same story but emphasised supposed German losses instead. One of the most colourful reports appeared in the local *Western Daily Press*:

[Bombers were met by] a heavy barrage from the ground defences, and RAF fighters took over to engage them. Several dogfights took place over the city and the noise of crashing bombs mingled with the roar of fighter engines, while flares and streams of tracer bullets coloured the moonlit sky.

As we have seen there had been night-fighters up, but few had been successful and those had been isolated combats rather than huge aerial battles. The newspapers emphasised that five German raiders were claimed destroyed.

In London, the details were equally sketchy and, at first, the scale of destruction was somewhat underestimated. There were, perhaps, 150 casualties in all. The damage was recognised as being widespread. The gasworks had suffered badly. There had been serious fires in the Midland Railway goods yard, in the west of the city, and at Crescent Gardens. The gas supplies were cut off but water and electricity should be alright. Railway traffic on the main Bristol to London route had to be diverted because of a damaged road bridge in Oldfield Park. The bomb had been one of the sequence that hit Stanley Road. However, all fires were under control and it was hoped that they would be extinguished by nightfall. Damage to residential property was substantial but 'little damage was done of national importance'.

Further information was difficult to collect. The telephones had broken down. Apsley House had supposedly taken a direct hit. As we have seen, this was not quite true. A near miss had caused some disruption and the decision had already been taken to move to the alternative headquarters at the Foresters Arms on Combe Down. Clearly the appropriate authorities had few beliefs that Bath was being raided because of her involvement with the Admiralty: the Foresters Arms public house stood opposite the main hutments at Foxhill, clearly marked on the German maps. Other Civil Defence parties moved from damaged depots. The Rescue Party at the Midland Bridge moved out to the playing fields at the Glasshouse. The ambulance post at St. James's Parade was not exactly damaged, but there had been an unexploded bomb there so they moved to the Homestead. When the various section heads met with the appropriate council officials of the Emergency Committee they could report that all Civil Defence services were functioning. However, the statistics were mounting up. Twenty fires were still burning. There were fifty-five known incidents. At least fifty people were dead, and 200 injured. There were well over 1,300 people at the various rest centres. Eight demolished houses were known to have people trapped there.

The statistics revealed a number of things. At the start of the war the expected death toll had been greatly overestimated. In common with other cities Bath had stockpiled large supplies of coffins. In the event, fewer people died; but far more were injured; and far, far more were rendered homeless and in need of some assistance. The aid from outside Bath had begun to pour in almost immediately. Indeed, so many crews had arrived at one depot during the lull that when the second raid began there was not enough room for all to shelter indoors. Some had to lie down outside. Ambulance and fire crews were particularly needed at first. The fire services had coped well. At present no fire was out of control. By evening the only ones still burning were those furthest from the main water supply, the river. Nor was there ever any real shortage of ambulances. Most first aid posts reported on the promptness with which casualties were picked up.

The great need now was for rescue parties. Skilled men were needed to find trapped people: men who knew how houses were built, and how they might collapse. However, large numbers were also needed to sift through the wreckage and to clear up the streets. Henry Hamlin, acting as temporary rescue depot leader, received rescue parties from the whole of north Somerset. Other units provided less skilled manpower to do the spade work. The Home Guard turned out in strength. Local army units sent in detachments. These created some minor problems. On site, rescue party leaders found they could not give orders directly to the soldiers but only via their NCOs. RAF Colerne, unable to do much to halt the night-time attack, did what it could in daytime by sending down a series of lorries with men and equipment.

The other great requirement was for people to provide food and comfort. There were many uninjured who, for various reasons, needed help. The vast influx of rescue workers also needed food and drink. Before the raids ended, the first call had gone out for mobile food supplies. The YMCA Queen's Messengers arrived. There were mobile kitchens, water tanks and canteens. It was later estimated that by 2.30 pm on Sunday, some 250 gallons of tea had already been served. The WVS set up a special canteen for rescue workers and the Fire Service. They served mugs of hot Oxo to wardens, Civil Defence workers and the bombed out.

Even so, there were still difficulties. Often, specialists were not replaced. The doctors worked without stopping. So did the undertakers at the emergency mortuaries. Even where replacement units did come in, it was difficult for local men to abandon work in areas that they knew well. Tom Gale had been fighting fires all night. He was relieved at 10.00 am Sunday, had a few hours rest and then went back to the station. Another fireman received large numbers of reinforcements but kept his men on duty so they could show the outsiders where to work. Despatch riders, performing the same task of guidance, had other problems. A number of motorbikes had come to grief on the previous night. Leslie Nott's had stopped temporarily when a wheel became entangled with fallen telegraph wires. By morning, the problems of driving through blacked out, rubble-strewn streets had led to a number of motorbikes being lost. William Harris, another motorbike rider, was sent to commandeer bikes from a shop in the city, Barton Motors. He took some six. Thus aided, the riders continued to guide new rescue parties to important incidents.

As soon as the second raid ended, the rescue work had begun. William Smith, one of the ambulance drivers, found that after the initial shock had worn off, people were coming to the depots and reporting that particular houses had been demolished. An ambulance would be sent. The first alarms were raised as certain people could not be found. Dr. Middlemas, of the Paragon, had not been seen since she went home during the lull. A few houses along, the sound of an explosion had been so loud that one man sheltering in his cellar thought that it was his house that had come down. When he emerged later, he discovered his house was quite intact. Dr. Middlemas's residence had been demolished. Kathleen Stainer, then a child, had taken cover all night. In the morning, one person had gone out and then returned with the words, 'You've seen pictures of it in the papers, now come out and see it for yourselves.'

Not all could come out and see. As dawn approached, several were still trapped, some being in a worse state than others. Hubert Jackson was still under his Morrison table shelter with the belief that most of the house was still standing:

Mr. Gay, a sergeant in the police, lived in the opposite house. He saw our house and walked over the debris, and said: 'Anybody there?'

'Yes, in the back room.'

He made his way around and eventually found his way to us and the window. I saw his silhouette. He crawled in and said: 'You alright?'

'Yes, we're fine, thank-you.'

'I'm glad to hear it.'

We didn't realise what had happened. He said:

'God you're in a mess here.' and we were told we had nothing left. 'No, Mr. Jackson, there's no house left.'

He let the side down on the shelter that could be let down. However, first he had to move some of the debris. When the roof came down the beams rested on the sill of the fireplace. This gave an angle under which he could move about in a hunched way.

A week before the blitz, my sister-in-law had sent her sewing machine. Mr. Gay had to move it a little roughly and my wife said:

'Be careful with it, you might do it some damage.'

It was already scratched and with all the house down as well, he was amused; but he apologised. He asked us what we were going to do. He said we couldn't move and suggested we wait till daylight. Then he would get the Home Guard. My wife had a dress in the shelter and put it on. We stayed there. Mr. Gay went off to report the incident. We stayed there until we heard voices again, the local Home Guard. We told them we were alright but we couldn't go the front door way. We had to go through the back gardens. They strung themselves out and passed my son along. We all got down somehow ... but there was a lot of dust about and when I left the Morrison, I was sick quite a lot. I pulled myself together. We weren't scratched at all.

It was relatively easy for the Jacksons to get out. So much of their house had been destroyed that it was largely just a case of opening up the wire of the shelter and getting over the rubble. In other houses, there was much more difficulty. Eric Davies was one such:

I could faintly see daylight, but there was no one around. Then came the all-clear. I heard footsteps come up the steps and a voice say:
'Anybody there?'
I don't know who it was. He walked on top of us. I felt it give and my neck felt tighter. I shouted and eventually they found us. They got my mother out first with the rubble falling off. I was the last out and wasn't sure whether I was coming or going. It was a beautiful morning.

Even so, there was a great deal of destruction. The house next door had been demolished. An old woman of 60 had been killed. Another house had practically burnt down. A third had lost its roof. But at least there were no further casualties. It took some time to extract the whole Davies family and in the resulting confusion, they went to a number of different hospitals:

I went to the Royal United Hospital, the RUH. There were bodies everywhere. There was a big crater near the Railway Hotel which had blown the whole road up. My wife had been taken out of the debris by the time I got out. Mum and dad had been taken out and when I got out the ambulances had already got them. I was told my wife and the rest of my family were in hospital. I found them there. My wife and baby were at one and my father at another. My mother had her vertebrae crushed. My father was the luckiest man alive. He had been sitting in a cheap fireside chair in the living room and could easily have been killed. He'd been blown out of his chair. He had a burn across the side of his head. He'd been thrown forward into the grate and he'd been trapped with his head on part of the top of the fire. He was practically on the surface, though. The doctor told me to take my shirt off. He said I'd be covered in bruises. I must have looked like a savage.

Doreen Wall had also been trapped in her parents' house as it caved in. Here the casualties were far more serious:

I remember sort of coming to and realising I was trapped. I couldn't move anything. There was wood above my head, but at least I could breathe. The bombs and machine-guns were still going. Then I heard the all-clear go. I didn't think we would be got out. Then there was lots of shouting and noise – the rescue squads and all were there. They had us all out. They pulled me out by the feet and I yelled because my left leg was all smashed up. My mother didn't survive. My father had a badly cut face and eye. We were also covered in plaster.

Doreen Wall and her father were taken on stretchers to a nearby garage. Here they waited for an ambulance to take them to the RUH. At the hospital they were laid down in a large room filled, it seemed, with shocked and dirty people. Eventually, Mrs. Wall was put into a bed, although no one knew exactly what was wrong with her leg. At St. Martin's, the other main hospital, Dr. Kohn was working non-stop. During the raids there were no operations. Skilled work was almost impossible when the area was under attack; and no one needed immediate surgery. Once the raids ended, Dr. Kohn never left the theatre. The ambulances arrived continually. At one point, Dr. Kohn received a telephone call from the Bristol Minister of Health. The doctor reported that he was running out of beds. The minister sent ten coaches over to pick up the old and chronically sick from St. Martin's. This emptied 100, much needed beds. Still, there was a great pressure on the nursing staff. Dr. Kohn felt they did a 'marvellous job'.

In many cases, those in hospital were the best looked after. The medical services had so many injured people to deal with that some of those with no physical wounds were left to themselves. Eric Davies had most of his family in hospital. He himself went down to the river with a bucket. Covered with plaster he had a good wash. Then he went off to have a couple of whiskies. Mr. Jackson and his family had been taken to the Moravian church hall in Coronation Avenue, a designated rest centre. Mr. Jackson did not stay long as he wanted to see what had happened. He returned to his house and walked amongst the debris. As he stood there, he heard a motorcycle and sidecar coming up the road. It was a colleague who had come to Ivy Grove to see that his landlady and relatives were safe:

> He asked if I was alright and where we were going. I hadn't thought about it. He said:
> 'Come with me.'
> I said he was only in rooms in Mount Road, but he said we had to sleep somewhere. I was ordered into the sidecar and pushed off with him. Later he got my wife and the boy and brought them up.

The fact that Hubert Jackson had given little thought to what to do next was symptomatic of the way some reacted. Most people suffered a degree of shock, whatever happened to them. The way to keep a grip of reality was to try and re-establish a routine. However, in the case of Mr. Jackson and others, the routine had been disturbed too much. His house had been destroyed; there was almost nothing to clear up. In such cases, it was easy to fall into a form of lethargy, a listlessness that prevented one from doing much to help oneself. Florence Delve was the last of those trapped on the first night whom we are considering. It was not very difficult for her to get out. The rescue services were not needed and all the neighbours had to do was to clear some rubble away. None of Mrs. Delve's family was even slightly injured. The scene was a mess, but the family was safe. Then came another tragedy:

> Next door lived two friends. They had a little girl who'd been

adopted by them six weeks before the raid. Jean, the girl, her mother was the niece of the two who adopted her. The mother lived in Swansea and had six children. Her husband was in the army and she lost sense of everything then. The children were picked up three times during the blitz there. Our friends adopted Jean. The mother agreed. There was some trouble and the girl had to go to the doctor's as her nerves were in pieces. After the first raid, they'd gone up to bed and taken Jean. She lay between them. The bomb fell and they came down with all of it. There were iron sides with the bed springs. One had gone through the mother's leg. Once we got out, we saw what had happened. Jean had just been dug out. My husband lifted her. She said: 'hello' and died. The only mark on her was a bruise on her forehead. Perhaps it was shock and what she'd been through. Her foster parents were very badly injured. I said the daughter was fine. What else could I say?

The two shocks of her house being destroyed and the death of her neighbour's child clearly affected Mrs. Delve:

We weren't injured at all. The first thing I heard was my baby crying. I tried to feed her but the shock had driven the milk away and I couldn't. I had never smoked till then but I was in such a state that my first husband told me to. My teeth were chattering. We never undressed and stayed in the same clothes until Wednesday night. You had to fend for yourself. It had stunned me so I couldn't think for myself. The last time I was safe was when I heard that whistle. From then on, it was a nightmare that I can only vaguely remember.

An ambulance came to remove the young girl's body that day. However, Mrs. Delve received no help. In her state she could do little for herself. Those who had suffered less, tended to recover more quickly: especially if they had a number of important, but containable, tasks to do. Cleaning up was one of the most common. A number of people who had taken shelter had first to find whether their houses had survived. One fireman, coming off duty, discovered his house had been badly damaged by incendiaries. Faith Dolman returned from Twerton Roundhill shelter to find her house completely intact. Not even the windows had been broken. Tony Self, a young boy, was actually disappointed. He had heard so much noise during the night that he expected to see much more destruction than he did when he looked out of the front door in the morning. Anne Marks left the basement in New King Street and returned to her parents' flat upstairs. All the china had been blown off the dresser, including Mrs. Marks' favourite antique cup. There was glass everywhere. When she looked out of the window she could see fires still burning in Oldfield Park. Also, the downstairs' wash-hand basin was sitting in an apple tree.

Few houses were completely flattened. Many had lost their weaker parts as a result of a blast nearby. Kathleen Stainer's house was a typical example. The roof tiles were haywire. All the glass had been blown in. Plaster had come off the interior walls. Mrs. Winifred Hurford had to cope with an invasion of hundreds of mice, presumably disturbed by the bombing. Ivy Hemingway spent a long time trying to clear up. Again, all the glass had gone. There was ceiling dust over everything, chunks of plaster in the toilet, the piano, the bath. She felt that everything was ruined. It was also still April, and bitterly cold in a windowless house. The fact that the gas was cut off did not help matters either. Kathleen Stainer boiled a kettle on a paraffin stove. Myrtle Meredith made porridge over a coal fire.

Some people were lucky enough to receive a visit from emergency repair men that day. They could do little more than first aid repairs for the time being. A number of houses had doors propped up or windows patched. Sam Hayward, the warden, helped board up his windows but this created an effect inside 'like the black hole of Calcutta'. James Webster returned to what was left of his home in Crescent Gardens.

He poked around. The fire had been so intense that there were melted icicles of lead hanging down from the roof. The house broke out in flames again on Sunday as fire had been smouldering deeper down. Other people were out as well. William Burden had been fire-watching at the Spa Hotel during the raids. In the morning he returned home:

> I went off duty at 8 am. I used to walk a lot and used to walk to the town centre and then catch a bus up to Devonshire Buildings. But there was no bus, so I had to walk. I went up Holloway. That was a mistake. It was practically blocked up solid. There was a lot of glass and Bath stone about. Many old dwelling houses in Holloway were just bricks and rubble. On the way up there, there were fire-pumps and trailers that had been working and there were bodies around them. By the time I got home I was walking on bricks, glass and slates.

Some people had homes to worry about; some had worries over relatives and friends as well. Mrs. Hayward was wondering where her husband, the special constable, had got to. Her sister-in-law, Doris Smith (no relation to the ambulance driver), with whom she was staying, tried to calm her nerves; perhaps her husband had had to go outside Bath for some reason. It was some time before it was announced he had been killed at the Scala shelter. Mr. Nott, the despatch rider, was concerned about his colleague, Wally Angus. He had no idea that Mr. Smith had already picked up the body:

> My deputy was Wally Angus, but we hadn't seen him and he hadn't signed on. After we got tidied up a bit, I sent someone to find him. As Brougham Hayes was blocked, he went the way of the Green Tree to where I said the bomb fell and saw his motorcycle there. One of the rescue services had collected various casualties from there by now. His wife had been contacted so she was worried. On Sunday afternoon we still couldn't find him. I had to go

round the mortuaries. I started at the Old Bridge. I then tried St. Peter's, but nothing. I picked up all the covers but there was nothing there. I reckon I turned at least 150 over. I tried Weston. Then I went out to Walcot. About the third I turned over from the last was Wally Angus. I don't know how they got him out there. His helmet was brought back to the station. The bomb had gone right along the road and a piece of shrapnel had gone through the helmet. It killed him instantly.

The ambulance drivers now had time to pick up bodies as well as the injured. Don Tuddenham took a number of bodies to the emergency mortuary in the crypt of St. James' Church in the centre of the city. Bodies were already being extracted from the Scala shelter and from Roseberry Road. Others came from Kingsmead. Still more were taken from King Edward Road, near the ruined church of St. Bartholomew. A Miss Meredith had some worries concerning this last area:

Next day, Sunday, was to have been our Sunday School anniversary and the church had been decorated accordingly, but of course, everything was ruined. Our schoolroom was a rest centre and able to be used although several windows were blown out. A special preacher had been booked to come from London, who stayed with certain church members and experienced a night of it! Being Sunday School secretary, I offered to take him over to Oldfield Park in the afternoon to meet our minister. We picked our way over the Windsor Bridge, which was in a fine mess, but on arriving at the minister's house, found it damaged and deserted, except for a billetee who advised us to go to the schoolroom rest centre. Here we found homeless people sitting around, and the minister's wife rendering first aid to a never ending queue of people. We then proceeded to King Edward Road where we found our man at a badly damaged house. A young lady had been pinned under a piano and was just being brought out on a stretcher. The two ministers greeted each other and had a few words. Then we walked to Weston.

The fact that it was Sunday robbed people of another form of routine – that of going to work. Jill Clayton's father went off to check that his haulage business was intact. Mrs Edith Gingell went to Walcot Parish church. Most of the windows had been blown out and it was rather draughty. There were not that many people present and they largely gathered together at the front. It was the first service to be held by the new rector, the Reverend Woodmansey. At present, he was still living in temporary accommodation at the Regina Hotel, near the Assembly Rooms. A Mrs. Lee, who was also at the Walcot church service remembers that the rector should have been officially 'read in' that day, but it was generally felt to be inappropriate. Instead of using the pulpit, he said a few words of comfort from the lectern in the body of the church. There was no service that evening.

Having tidied up, found relatives, checked businesses or gone to church, most people found there was little more for them to do. As they gathered together, stories were soon being spread. It was a phenomenon found in other raids that, after initial shock and worry, there would be an excess of emotion. People would show great excitement and tell a great number of stories. Mrs. Marks was disappointed that the end of Kingsmead Street had been closed off. Neighbours were full of stories, of girls cut down by machine-guns, of deaths in this house, of the destruction of others. Most took it for granted that there would be another raid on Sunday evening. Once tasks had been done and stories told, this prospect was the dominant theme. Some felt they had to leave the city, even if it meant no more than walking to just outside the city boundaries and, preferably, staying with friends. Some had no choice. Mr. Webster, his house burnt, went out to friends at Bathford. Betty Tutt went to Bradford-on-Avon. Anne Marks went to stay with her grandmother just outside Bath.

Edwin Stainer, then a child, remembers that his uncle came

round to his parents' house. After some time he convinced Mr.
Stainer's mother that the whole family should leave that night.
They all went out to Hampton Rocks, above Bathampton. On
the opposite side of the valley, at Brown's Folly, were Mark
Whiteley and his family. Some people did not go out so far.
Mr. Davies went to Southstoke, to the Pack Horse public
house, but found it was already full up. Luckily a friend of
his wife lived nearby and she provided shelter. The need to
get away led some to choose the most unlikely refuge. Doris
Smith was sister to Mr. Hayward, the special constable who
had been killed at the Scala:

> A neighbour was a railwayman on the Somerset and Dorset.
> On the second night we went with him and took a thermos
> flask and some sandwiches to the Combe Down tunnel.
> We stood outside until the sirens went. We didn't know if
> the trains were still running. I went in with my little girl. I
> was terrified that a train might come. There were alcoves in
> the tunnel we could have stood in, but there were no trains
> that night.

Some were very anxious to leave the city. Rosalind Field left
in the evening with her brother-in-law who had come across
from Bristol to collect her. They caught one of the last buses
out of the city, a lucky chance as 'some people were panicking
a bit'. The local authorities helped to arrange a degree of
organised evacuation. Some 1,500 people had gathered in
the rest centres by Sunday morning, with nowhere else to go.
It was essential that they were evacuated. If they stayed in
the centres and a bomb hit one, then casualties could be very
high indeed. Jill Clayton remembers going with her mother to
an army camp that was taking in people. A few people were
forced to move. Mrs Emily Coleman lost all the windows in
her house on the first night. She went round to her parents in
Widcombe. At about 9.00 pm the police called to ask whether
the house would be occupied that night. The family answered
in the affirmative and were then told they would have to move.

There was an unexploded bomb at the top of the road.

Most people stayed. Again, some had no choice. Doreen Wall could hardly move from her hospital bed. Some stayed because elderly relatives could not really move. Faith Dolman knew that her grandmother could hardly be expected to take a long walk out of the city and sleep rough. A Mrs. Muse, who lived on Beechen Cliff, remembers her parents taking in her grandparents, after they had been bombed out from the Lower Bristol Road on the previous night. Many did not fancy spending a cold April night lying out in a field, or wanted to stay and look after their houses. Faith Dolman went along to the Roundhill shelter again. So did Hubert Jackson, now staying with friends in Mount Road. Mrs. Delve, still too shocked to do much, took cover in a horse's shed in Kingswood Gardens at the top of Primrose Hill. Conversely, some stayed because their areas had not suffered badly on the first night. Muriel Gough, having spent the first night at the Salvation Army hostel, bedded down in her parents' Morrison shelter in Kingston Road.

Mrs. Dolman had watched some people carrying their bedding out towards Englishcombe. Sam Hayward, in Oldfield Park, saw people in that area going up the road and crossing those who lived in Weston going in the opposite direction. An elderly neighbour asked if he was leaving:

> One old lady, Mrs. Bridges, who was about 80, asked me if I was leaving. I said 'no' – I was going to protect my house. She said: 'Thank God. I shall know if anything happens, you can look after me.' I never got up when the sirens went. If your name was on the bullet, you'd get it.

Apart from the stoicism, it was a good thing that Mr. Hayward did stay. After all, he was a warden. The authorities in other areas had often had mixed views about people leaving the city, 'trekking' as it was often called. It might reduce the casualties and get rid of a large number of 'useless mouths'. However, in some cases, essential personnel were choosing to leave the city. On the first night a number of wardens had had problems when householders left without tackling their own incendiaries. As more houses were left vacant on the second night, the potential danger increased still further. The problem was greatly exacerbated when the fire-watchers themselves left the city. Fire-watching was rarely a popular occupation: one night in three, perhaps, spent awake in some public building and after a full day's work too. Absences were not uncommon. On the first night of the raid, Miss Meredith had sheltered with a young couple. The husband should have been fire-watching at his place of work but had not gone after, he claimed, eating some bad peas. It is impossible to estimate how many people did leave the city that night but certainly the figure ran into thousands. With pardonable overstatement, one later report recorded,

'It is the general feeling that the Fire Guard largely disintegrated after the first raid.'

That there were noticeably fewer people in Bath by Sunday evening is certainly true. When Faith Dolman went along to the Roundhill shelter, she found that it was only half full. It had been packed on the previous night. Even those people who stayed were expecting another raid. Mrs. Dolman awaited it with a mixture of fear and interest. Few went to bed and even fewer bothered to remove their day clothes. Most settled down in their shelters. Kathleen Muse, with parents and other relatives, bedded down in their Morrison. Muriel Gough and her family did the same.

The Civil Defence personnel made preparations as well. A number of depots and a fair amount of equipment were moved to the outskirts to avoid being hit, or trapped, if the city centre was attacked again. However, the city was not surrounded by Civil Defence teams. There might be a raid on Bath, it might be elsewhere. Bristol and other local areas were on stand-by but there was no point in stationing equipment in a city where it might get destroyed; and when it might be needed in some other location. Nor were all the Bath crews available. Some were exhausted. Tom Gale, his lungs affected by the Roseberry Road blast, was not fit for active fire-fighting. He was put in charge of one of the section Fire Stations. Yet there were sufficient fire pumps and ambulances; the depot and posts were manned. In theory, reinforcements could be rushed into Bath as soon as they were required and called for. The city awaited another attack.

CHAPTER EIGHT

Sunday: Raid Three

During the whole of Sunday, the local RAF squadrons had been making their preparations as well. 87 Squadron spent its time getting as many aircraft serviceable as possible. 125 Squadron went a stage further. The Beaufighter was too much of a novelty to be used efficiently. As a result, the pilots temporarily borrowed some of the older, but more familiar, Defiants and Hurricanes. These, also, had to be serviced very quickly. The squadron adopted new tactics. The policy of 'Fighter Night' was frequently adopted when the target could be predicted, as on this second night. This meant putting up a series of fighters at given, different altitudes over the target city. No other friendly aircraft would be allowed within twenty miles of the city centre; so any aircraft seen could be taken to be a hostile one. The first of 87 Squadron's aircraft took off at 11.25 pm. By midnight, there was a standing patrol of Hurricanes and Defiants over the Bath area.

The weather conditions on Sunday night were for the most part cloudless. Over south-west England and north-west France the visibility was only moderate to poor. At some time before 01.00 am, the first of 83 German bombers took off for another attack on Bath. They crossed the English coast on a wide front between the Isle of Wight and Torquay. At 01.06 am the anti-aircraft guns at Portland opened fire, to little effect. At the same time the first aerial contact with an intruder was made. Once again, 307 Squadron from Exeter claimed an early success. One of their Beaufighters had been on patrol for three hours, since 10.00 pm. The pilot was having difficulty with his oxygen equipment and finally made a request to return to base. At the very same moment he was informed that ground radar had picked up a contact: an enemy aircraft was approaching the Devon coast from the south-east. At 01.14 am a visual was obtained, a Junkers 88 silhouetted in front of the moon. The Beaufighter closed to within a few hundred yards before opening fire. The results were dramatic. The two second burst may have killed most of the crew. Perhaps it put the rudder out of action. The bomber made an uncontrolled half roll to port. It almost collided with the attacker before falling away rapidly. The Beaufighter's AI radar tracked it down until it seemed to hit the sea near Hope Cove. A second JU.88 was attacked by another of 307 Squadron's night-fighters. Strikes were seen along the fuselage, but contact was then lost.

The air raid sirens sounded in Bath at 01.15 am. The defending fighter squadrons had rather more success this time. 87 Squadron produced two encounters over the city with its Hurricanes. Neither was conclusive. Flight Sergeant Trybulec opened fire at a Dornier 17. He did not see the results as he was dazzled by the flash of his guns. Another Hurricane, flown by Pilot Officer Grantham, was flying over Lansdown. Grantham was not alone. He was flying in tandem with a converted Havoc aircraft which had a large searchlight mounted on its nose. The idea was that the radar in the Havoc would pick up a contact. The searchlight would illuminate it for the accompanying fighter. In practice the system was rarely a success; in this case, it was not needed. Grantham saw his target when an overconfident bomber sprayed machine-gun fire along the ground. The tracer bullets were easily seen. At 01.40 am the Hurricane opened fire and, although a visual was lost, the plane was claimed damaged.

125 Squadron had a more varied evening. The first contact was again because a German acted somewhat thoughtlessly. At 02.00 am another bomber, this time a Dornier 17, was seen firing down onto the ground. Wing Commander Ivins in his Hurricane closed to within 200 yards from the rear before opening fire. The bomber was hit on the right wing and starboard engine. But the Wing Commander suddenly felt his engine cut off as he failed to throttle back. He passed over the damaged bomber and lost contact. A quarter of an hour later a Defiant from the same squadron saw a Heinkel's tracer bullets some twenty miles south-west of Bath. Then the aircraft could be seen silhouetted against the moon. The Defiant fired a two second burst into the bomber. A piece flew off and the fuselage glowed. The Heinkel dived downwards and

was claimed as probably destroyed. Another 125 Squadron Defiant encountered a Heinkel some five minutes later. The bomber itself launched the attack which should have been a fatal mistake. Assuming its opponent to be a front-firing Hurricane, the Germans attacked from above and behind. But the Defiant had a rear-firing gun turret. The Defiant's gunner could hardly believe his luck. He held his fire until the last moment. He pressed the triggers. Nothing happened. Luckily, the bomber's fire was wildly inaccurate. It was only when the Defiant's crew returned to base that they discovered the guns could not be fired. The firing safes had not been fitted. There had been such a rush to prepare aircraft for Sunday night, that a number were bound to produce mechanical faults.

A number of aircraft were hit elsewhere. At 01.39 am one wandered too near the Bristol anti-aircraft defences. Eight rounds were fired and a glow was seen in the sky. The bomber descended in flames a minute later. Another aircraft was claimed by anti-aircraft fire further south, just under an hour later. Along the coast and over Exmoor, two more bombers were attacked but with little result. Once again, the bombing effort was not always concentrated. Amongst others, Crediton and Bridport were bombed. Cardiff anti-aircraft guns opened fire for a short time; but the German air attack was no minor effort; nor was it hindered to any great extent. Over Bath two aircraft had been claimed damaged, one probably destroyed. All had depended on visual sightings rather than radar. The German bombers had been seen only when silhouetted against the moon or because they were using their machine-guns. 307 Squadron claimed one destroyed. Anti-aircraft batteries claimed two. Most, therefore, again escaped without any damage whatsoever.

All this meant very little, at present, to the people on the ground. Many trekkers had stopped as soon as they were out of the immediate vicinity of Bath. Some, therefore, had a good view of the bombing. Mark Whiteley, at Brown's Folly, could see the bombs exploding in the east of the city. It was a more overcast evening than the first and at times the flames could be seen reflected in the clouds. Explosions were clearly visible. Mrs. Marks, at her grandmother's home just outside Bath, stood in the garden. She watched the glow of the fires over the city and wondered if her father, still working there, was safe. Eric Davies, in the woods near Southstoke, was one of the nearest to the city. He quite plainly saw the bombers in twos and threes heading for the burning city centre.

Those who stayed in Bath faced another harrowing night. One family had the worst of both worlds. Expecting a second night of raids, they had gathered their bedding and camped at the edge of the city. But it was extremely cold and by midnight it seemed the Germans were not coming. They decided to walk home again. They had been home for only a few minutes when the sirens sounded and they left the house and sprinted to the nearby field. No one treated this siren as a false alarm. Mrs. Selwyn and her colleagues at the Homestead First Aid Post were more frightened than ever. The first raid had taken people by surprise; now they knew what might happen. Florence Delve was with her first husband in an arched stable. Considering their recent experiences it was no surprise that nerves were a little frayed and might snap at any moment:

> Many people came up from town to the stable. It was an arch and you could see all of Weston fields. The Germans were machine-gunning all down the edges. You could see the guns. We knew there were people in the fields but we couldn't get any more in our shelter. One man struck a match to light a cigarette. My husband hit him for six, saying: 'You light another bloody match and I'll hit you to the crown. You call yourself a bloody soldier.' This was only to be expected when you'd lost your home.
>
> (Florence Delve)

One group of people who had already suffered and had no chance to move, were those in hospital. Doreen Wall was at the RUH:

SUNDAY: RAID THREE

My ward was full. I thought I couldn't get out of bed so I just put my head under the bedclothes. Even the nurses took cover under the beds, popping up to see if we were alright. It was very frightening. Combe Park took it badly. I remember seeing some houses, through the window, on fire although there was no damage done at the RUH.

St. Martin's hospital had a closer shave. Mary Nott was there, telephoning for transport to get her to her post. One aircraft passed overhead and circled around the hospital before dropping a stick of fire bombs. It then machine-gunned along Wellsway as it headed for the centre of the town. Luckily the bombs landed in fields rather than on the hospital opposite. A near miss was sufficient to wreck the X-ray equipment though, and a mobile unit had to be brought in. Mrs. Nott, having observed the attack, looked around for the friends she had just been talking to. They had taken cover behind a wall. She had remained standing, watching the German bombers.

In fact, once the raid began many people were calmer than on the first night: albeit usually those who had been relatively unscathed. If they had survived one night, why not a second? Mrs. Dolman, at the Roundhill shelter, felt there was far less panic this second time. At the Homestead First Aid Post, casualties were much calmer than on the previous night. On the Saturday evening there had been a great deal of shock. The toilets were in continual use. There was much vomiting. On Sunday only two young women who were bombed out displayed signs of hysterical weeping. One had been dug out of the passage of a collapsed house. More worrying was the number of minor injuries, including people from the rescue services themselves. A number had sprains – ankles and the like. Too many people had had too little sleep and were getting injured as a result.

All of the first aid posts were hindered at times by having to work in the dark. The Homestead had a near miss. Marjorie Horsell remembers that the post literally 'danced'; this blew in the windows and blackout curtains. Until these had been put up again, lights had to be turned off. For two hours the staff had to work with the light of torches. Once again, the Civil Defence organisation itself was under attack. The Control Centre had moved from Apsley House to the Foresters Arms. This possessed fewer facilities. Also, not everyone realised that the centre had moved and as a result many of the messages were sent to the police headquarters instead. In the event, soon after the raid started most of the telephone network was knocked out once again. Other posts were in trouble as well. On the first night St. James's Parade had received an unexploded bomb. This time another bomb landed that did explode. It was a stroke of good fortune that the entire personnel had been evacuated. Two ambulances were lost, however, when the workshop collapsed. Elsewhere, the Rescue Service lost six vehicles in a burn out when an incendiary bomb ignited petrol.

Early in the Sunday raid, one other type of Civil Defence depot was damaged; and this might have been a major tragedy. The rest centres had filled up on Saturday night but had been evacuated as soon as possible on the following day. Now, as the bombs fell again, more people were forced to turn to them. One was at West Twerton School:

When I heard the siren, I went there to escape and to find some company. A bomb landed in the road. The other side of the school got the worst. Some were killed. I couldn't get out of the door. The wall came down. I was shocked. My sister couldn't talk at all. There was glass everywhere. One boy had lots of glass in his head. They finally managed to loosen the stones to get us out. There was a bomb at the back which killed one man. His wife was calling to see her husband although she knew he was dead. Even the wardens were running wild. One little girl was blown out through the window and was found on the pavement. It was very sad. I didn't quite realise what was happening.

(Rose Miller)

A German Air Force photo-map of Bath: the Admiralty hutments at Foxhill (A) and the gasworks (B) are marked. The word 'Bath' is written across the Kingsmead area. *(Bath City Council)*

Preamble to disasters to follow: On Good Friday 1941 a lone German bomber dropped four bombs on the Dolemeads area of Widcombe. Eleven people died.

The Assembly Rooms on fire on the night of Sunday 26 April, after incendiaries caught the roof alight. The fire brigade ran out of water and stood by helplessly.

Above: Abbey Church House.
Below: A new view of Bath Abbey seen through the wreckage of No 38 Wellsway.

The Regina Hotel on Bennett Street near the Circus. Many guests ignored warnings to go to the basement shelter and died when the building received a direct hit.

Kingsmead Street. Severely damaged on both nights of the raids, much of Kingsmead Street was demolished and has not been rebuilt. It is now the site of a car park.

New King Street. Destruction caused by one of a stick of bombs that fell early in the first raid. The Ford family, mother and six children, died here.

Albion Place, Lower Bristol Road. Below, on fire during the Saturday night raid and, above, sightseeing on Sunday morning. Now replaced by a car showroom.

Above and below: Fires burn in the Upper Bristol Road early in the Saturday raid.

Above: Julian Road well alight on the night of 25/26 April.
Below: With the rubble cleared from the roads Bathonians go about their business.

Above and below: near Harley Street. The fronts of houses torn off by bomb blast. Paintings still hang on the walls. Firemen damp down the rubble on Sunday morning.

Nos 28-30 The Paragon were completely destroyed during the raids of Saturday night. The bodies of Dr. Mary Middlemas, her sisters Elsie and Jean and their two maids, Freda Baker and Edna Hawkins, were recovered from the ruins on the following Wednesday. It appears that they were trapped by debris following the bombing and were burnt to death. Dr. Middlemas had earlier been on duty at the Snow Hill first aid post.

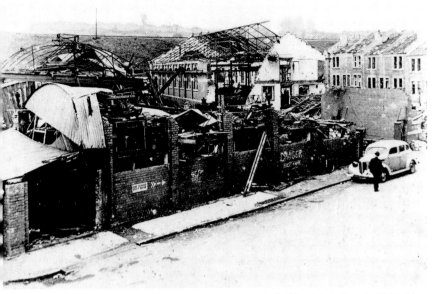

Scenes of destruction at the Stanley engineering works in Monkdale Road, Oldfield Park. Despite extensive damage the factory was repaired and restored to production.

Above: St. James', gutted by fire on Sunday night. Below: St. Andrew's, Julian Road damaged by bombs on Saturday and destroyed by incendiaries on Sunday.

Above: Collapsed houses in Shakespeare Avenue.
Below: Wholesale destruction in Manvers Street.

Above: Unexploded bomb near Churchill House, Dorchester Street.
Below: Roseberry Road, a near miss − intended for the gasworks?

Above: West Twerton School – a schoolboy's dream come true!
Below: Street shelters survived the blast in Stanley Road West, Oldfield Park.

Above: Dad's Army guards the ruins of The Bank of England.
Below: Smith Brothers Wine Vaults, No 11 Westgate Buildings.

Above: Shops destroyed in Hayes Place, Bear Flat.
Below: The People's Mission, Somerset Street, half demolished by a 500kg bomb.

Above: Temporary repairs under way in Oldfield Park.
Below: Marlborough Lane. Two houses were destroyed and six seriously damaged.

Above: King Edward Road. Note the street shelters that survived the blast.
Below: The north side of Victoria Road, Brougham Hayes.

Above: Nos 16 and 17 King Edward's Road.

Below: No 83 Oldfield Park completely destroyed by blast.

Above: Houses destroyed at the junction of Holloway and Magdalen Road.
Below: Civil Defence workers dig into the rubble of a demolished house.

Above and below: Salvaging personal property from bombed-out homes.

Above: The Fire Service gets supplies of water from the fountain in Laura Place.
Below: A mobile field kitchen providing food for the homeless.

Above: An emergency mobile laundry.
Below: An elderly resident being rescued from her bombed-out home.

Above: Sharing water with a smile.
Below: Children play on a bomb site in Julian Road.

Above: Two 1,000kg bombs struck Elm Grove Terrace. Little survived.
Below: There were many human scenes like this after the bombardment.

Above: King George VI and Queen Elizabeth chatting with Bath residents.
Below: The first mass funeral at Haycombe Cemetery.

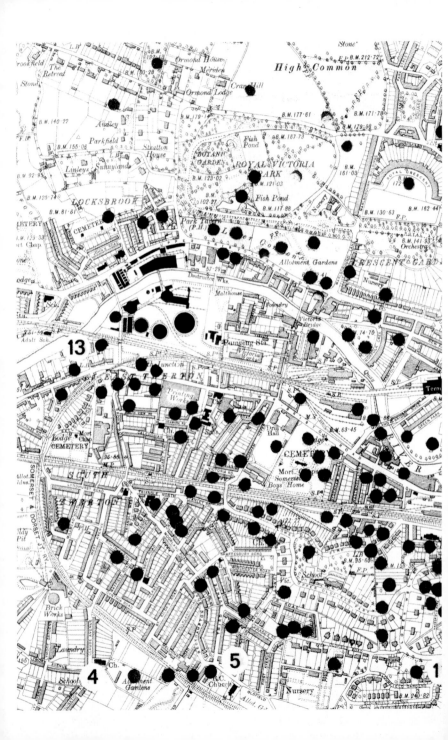

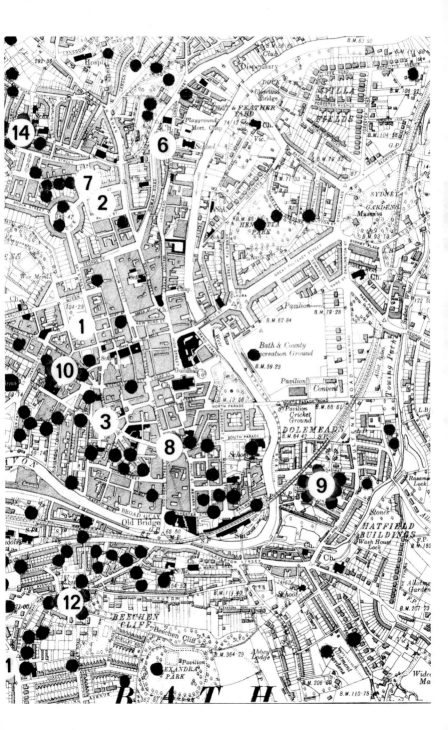

Above: Tea, Britain's traditional answer to problems, was dispensed in gallons after the raids; in this case from a YMCA canteen.

Below: The former labour exchange, severely damaged during the raids and still bearing the scars, is listed Grade II.

SUNDAY: RAID THREE

Vic Penny, the ambulance driver, was sent to the scene. He tried three or four routes before he found a clear road. When he arrived there were already a number of ambulances at the scene. Some people were shocked. But although there were deaths, they were relatively few because it was not a direct hit. Casualties in general during this third raid were quite low. Other rest centres were able to cope with the homeless, although a number more were to be damaged before the end of the evening. Bath's Civil Defence faced one more problem. On Saturday night the raid had not been expected. Once it occurred the regional headquarters at Bristol had responded promptly to calls for aid. On Sunday much was promised; but for some reason there was a delay in its arrival. Bath had three rescue squads ready at the start of the raid. Bristol had promised seven further squads if another raid did occur. In the event, these did not arrive immediately and the three local squads were left to deal with at least fifteen incidents. Fire Brigade units were also not sent as quickly as they might. This was a great pity considering the nature of the bombings on the second night.

On Saturday, the Germans had first dropped incendiary bombs, largely to illuminate the target. This had been followed by high-explosives. These tore houses and other buildings apart. In theory, the inflammable contents of the houses would then be exposed. The inhabitants might have fled this onslaught. In these circumstances, there was scope for a further incendiary attack. It was later estimated that 4½ tons of incendiary bombs were dropped during the raids, and most of these fell on the second night. Some additional fires were caused by tracer bullets. Within a short time of the Sunday raid starting, there were numerous small fires; and two areas in which major conflagrations were developing. One was, yet again, Kingsmead. A later report claimed that on the first night the bombers had flown on a west-east axis. On the second they had gone north-south. The two paths crossed over Kingsmead Square. Within an area bounded by Green Park Buildings, Monmouth Street, Kingsmead Square and Kingsmead Lane, several acres of buildings came under concentrated and sustained attack. Ron Taylor and his father were on the roof of their house again trying to prevent burning brands from setting their home alight. At one point they had to ask firemen in the streets below to direct their hoses onto their roof. Nearby, in Kingsmead Street, Fullers Garage had been burning for some time. Suddenly it exploded, sending tyres and other fittings hundreds of feet into the air. It may have been a direct hit. Perhaps petrol had ignited. Holy Trinity Church, hit on the first night, was gutted by fire on the second. A bomb landed near the newly built Labour Exchange, severely pitting the front of the building. The blast also hit a public shelter a mere four yards away. All that happened was that the sandbagged end of the shelter was blown away. Its inhabitants remained intact. The Labour Exchange had more damage inflicted upon it. Two stories high, its roof of slates and boarding caught alight when incendiaries fell on top of it. The two fire-watchers detailed to watch the building were both rather old and, not surprisingly, taking shelter. As a result, the whole top storey burnt down.

Nearby were the three wings of the new Kingsmead Flats. The roof of one wing, Kingsmead East, caught fire, but the Fire Service prevented this from spreading. A few hundred yards to the west stood the two wings of Green Park, terraced Georgian houses. Within a short time a complete wing of some 30 houses had caught fire. The fire was fanned by a strong east wind but to spread as far as it did suggests that there were few people available to stop it. One house, in the middle of the row, did survive, although the houses on either side went up in flames. In that house a caretaker, who happened to be a trained fireman, succeeded in extinguishing the fire in his roof with the aid of a stirrup-pump. Other people were around trying to stop the fires, but at crucial times they were driven to take cover by German machine-gunning.

Nevertheless, the Fire Guard situation was far from satisfactory. It had never been popular: indeed, the idea of ordering people to guard unoccupied buildings had only come about because a voluntary system did not work. Fire-watchers had no uniforms, no real common unity. It had often been thought a waste of time. A Heads of Services survey in Bath after the raids felt that the Fire Guards had stood up well during the first night's bombing. However, on the second night many had left the city and the job of fire prevention was left to the wardens and local help. Others found that many buildings had been locked up. A number of factories had had no one on duty at all, or just people watching from the roofs. The Theatre Royal received some damage from incendiary bombs. However, these were extinguished by a fortuitous chance. The Sadler's Wells ballet had come down for a series of performances starting that Saturday. A number of their lodgings had been damaged, so some of the troupe had left and slept in the theatre itself, and thus helped to save it from burning. The fire watching problem was not confined to public buildings. Many people openly admitted that they left their houses as soon as incendiary bombs landed on them. Yet small fires could be smothered if dealt with promptly.

This applied not only to incendiary bombs. Blast could do strange things. In one large house there were two families. One went out of Bath that evening. The other stayed. On the Sunday night a near miss blew coals out from the fire. If one family had not stayed at home and put this fire out then the whole house might have burned down. A Mr. Wick had to deal with a similar case in his house when a bomb drew the fire out of the grate. In another case, a house had its windows blown in. This also removed the blackouts while the lights stayed on. If there had been no one around to turn them off, then a well-lit house would have become an obvious target. This is not to write off the entire Fire Guard. Many did excellent work. It was no easy thing to leave one's family and go to guard a building in which one had, possibly, very little interest. It was even more difficult to stay there when the bombs were falling and one was worried for oneself and one's family elsewhere. Some died at their duty. A Mr. Self was killed while on duty at Kingsmead School. Bernard Humphries' father worked as a cabinet maker for Lock's furniture works on Lower Bristol Road. On the first night he had been fire-watching there. A direct hit had blown him into the river. When he crawled out he found the factory had been blown away. However, many people did leave before the second raid. At least one person returned to find their home razed to the ground the following morning. Perhaps this might not have happened had they stayed.

With the best will in the world, the sheer concentration of bombs in the Kingsmead area would have defied all but the most determined Fire Guards. In the other, if smaller, conflagration near Bath Spa railway station there were peculiar difficulties. The area possessed a large number of inflammable buildings. Long and Sons, the builders, had a timber roof. The Salvation Army hostel had only a wooden roof. A nearby dairy, of more modern construction, still had just a matchboard roof. All were set alight by incendiaries. Luckily the hostel had been cleared of the homeless during the day. To tackle these fires was difficult in any circumstances; but it was almost impossible when incendiaries were mixed in with a fair number of high-explosive bombs. One fell on the platform and rails of Bath Spa station itself. It tore up the platform, four sets of rails and demolished St. John's Church house killing two people, including a clergyman. Another four or five landed in the back roads in the area. One fell in Kingston Road:

My father said that my mother, the two girls and I should sleep in the (Morrison) shelter. We had a mattress and pillows. My father and brother were upstairs. When the sirens went, there was an old man who lived on his own. My father fetched him and two people and their little girl from next door. We had three sides of the wire up ... we pulled up the fourth side. The little girl had just got down with the old chap and were coming into the shelter. There was a colossal crash. My mother said to get in quick but there was no time. The next bomb hit us. The old chap was caught by the wire on his legs as he was blown into the shelter. It was pitch dark. I thought my neck was broken as I had been thrust forward. There was panic for about a minute as we were too crowded. My father was very level-headed. He said we should all be quiet. No one could see. There were bombs all around. I had had a bicycle lamp in my hand but it had been blown away. We felt around, and it was on a pillow. So we had a light to see. But all we knew was that we were trapped. It seems that the bomb fell at 1.15 am as our watches all stopped then. We anticipated that when the all-clear went we'd be found immediately. But this wasn't so. It seems that the wardens moved all of the people out to the Parade Gardens' shelters.

(Muriel Gough)

Other areas suffered attack from fire, although the incidents were mostly isolated. The raids were one of the first major tests of the reorganised National Fire Service. The earlier local system had worked well, but heavy air raids had pointed out a number of weaknesses. Bombs could easily smash or rupture the water mains. Reinforcements from other areas might arrive in a city and find that their hoses did not fit the local hydrants. To some extent the equipment was standardised for the NFS. However, the main innovation was a series of ways to ensure a continual supply of water. Two, in particular, were used in Bath. A large number of static tanks were built. These were, in many cases, no more than metal tanks sunk into the ground and filled with water. One stood at the west end of Royal Crescent. The second device was the laying of emergency mains. These were six inch steel piping laid on the surface and connecting static tank to static tank. These stood up far better to explosives, even though they were on the surface, than the cast iron mains. Bath had three such pipelines linking tanks at the top of the city with the river below. The city also had three fire-boats to deal with fires near the river.

In the event, a number of things went wrong. Like the Rescue Services, the Fire Brigade reinforcements were very slow in arriving at times. Outside crews, when they did arrive, could still have ill-fitting equipment. Reinforcements were hampered by the fact that the Upper Bristol Road was blocked and they had to enter the city by other routes. They frequently got lost in the city. Few had any idea where the static tanks were located. This became extremely important. Within half an hour of the raid beginning, high-explosive bombs had wrecked the mains. The mains supply had been cut in half. One, possibly two, of the fire-boats had already been sunk on the first night. Two of the three overground pipelines had been hit. One was completely shattered. The other was peppered by bomb splinters. Especially in areas far from the river, the statics often became the only real supply of water; and a tank was only a limited source of water that could soon dry up. Furthermore, the roads became increasingly difficult to drive through. They were blocked not only by masonry and timber, but also by steel girders, window frames, bricks, broken glass and telephone wires. Nor was the control station exempt. The Fire Brigade's Divisional Headquarters at Number 3, Royal Crescent, temporarily ceased to function when a near miss blew in the blackout curtains.

For a variety of reasons, therefore, some units of the NFS could not deal with some fires. On a number of occasions, they seemed to take a very long time to arrive, Stothert & Pitt was a case in point. If the Germans were to claim they were attacking a military target in Bath, then this was the place to mention. On two separate sites various military aids were made; in particular tank mountings and one-man submarines. On the first night one particularly large bomb had wrecked a shed building at the Victoria Works. It had also peeled the roof off another shed. Unfortunately the lights had remained on. William Delve, who worked there, had had to go along and knock them all off with a hammer.

On the second night it was the turn of the Newark Works. A four-storey office block had lost most of its windows on the Saturday due to a near miss. It had also had a number of incendiaries but these had been extinguished by the extremely efficient brigade that the works provided itself. However, on

Sunday night the members of the regular works brigade were either taking a well earned rest or looking after their own bombed-out families. Only relatively untrained personnel were on duty. The German policy of blasting buildings open with high-explosives first, to lay open the inflammable contents, paid dividends. Flying burning brands set a small wooden hut alight. Flames from this fire ignited the blackout curtains which were flapping outside the broken office windows. The fire-fighters discovered that their single trailer pump was ineffective; its suction hose had been damaged by bomb fragments. No one knew where the spare was kept. In desperation, they sought help from the Fire Service. The telephones did not work. They tried to find transport to go to get help; but the only van available was sitting in the garage. Its brake was off and it had rolled against the door, effectively jamming it. By the time the door had been forced, both the van and another car had been destroyed by fire. The general manager had to run a couple of miles to the Fire Station. Several times on the way he had to take cover. Not until 80 minutes after he left for help did the Fire Service arrive. By that time the office block was well ablaze. The fire was also spreading to the more important main machine shop. Luckily the firemen were able to prevent this fire from spreading further. The office block was gutted however.

The most famous loss came on the second night, and far from the river. The Assembly Rooms had only been reopened in 1938 after many years of neglect. Incendiary bombs set the roof alight. It is said that the Fire Brigade arrived in plenty of time. They had the fire completely under control and contained within a very small part of the building. Apparently the water then ran out. The fire crews could do nothing more but stand and watch. Within a short time most of the inside had been gutted. Only the Card Room, Club Room and Restaurant Kitchen remained intact. This area north of the river suffered badly during the Sunday raid. Julian Road had a number of fires. The area just behind the Royal Crescent went up in flames. On the triangle there stood St. Andrew's Church.

Incendiaries caught its roof on fire as well. Vic Penny, the ambulance driver, remembers driving along Julian Road. He could see the church blazing away and firemen with hoses.

Another church was burned down that night. At St. James' a thanksgiving service had been held on Sunday. Bodies had been taken to the crypt which served as an emergency mortuary. Once again, it was the roof that caught fire. At one point Mr. Penny was still taking bodies into the crypt while firemen were trying to extinguish the flames in the top of the building. Much of the water eventually ran into the cellar. Some of the bodies began to float around. As Mr. Penny watched, one of the bells crashed down into the body of the church. A gallery came down close to a number of firemen. One was burnt badly on the hip. The wound later turned to gangrene. Yet despite all the dangers, only one fireman appears to have died that night. He was working in the Circus when a bomb fell nearby. He looked up at the wrong moment and a piece of shrapnel killed him.

St. James' was the only major fire in the centre of the city. It was an isolated case. In Southgate Street a potential disaster was smothered by the prompt work of a couple of fire-watchers. Although the fire bombs were very destructive of property, they tended to create few casualties and people could run from fire. The area near the railway station was largely burned out. A number of high-explosive bombs had landed, including the one that destroyed Muriel Gough's house. Yet casualties remained mercifully low: many had evacuated or taken proper precautions to take cover. But there were a number of serious incidents involving high-explosive bombs and severe loss of life as well.

Two hotels were hit and both were half demolished. In Queen Square the Francis Hotel lost 26 yards of its frontage. The blast was sufficient to send fragments flying across the square which embedded themselves in the northern side, some 100 yards away. A number of the ill-starred Sadler's Wells company had been staying at the hotel. With most of the other guests, they had taken shelter in the basement.

They survived, but most of the musical instruments left in their rooms were never seen again. A number of people were trapped in the basement for a while but because they had taken cover, casualties were relatively low. Perhaps five people died. At the Regina Hotel, opposite the ill-fated Assembly Rooms, the situation was far worse. It seems that when the siren sounded most of the staff and guests went down to the specially strengthened basement. As luck would have it, the shelter stood under the half of the hotel that was not hit. But a number of guests decided to stay in their rooms. The bomb that destroyed the left half of the hotel killed many of these people. Some were crushed to death by falling masonry. Some 30 people were killed. Amongst them was the Reverend Woodmansey, the new vicar of Walcot church.

One area received a large number of high-explosive bombs. The area south of the river from Holloway and Beechen Cliff to Bear Flat had suffered some damage on the first night. On the second it was hit by even more bombs. Most of the Victorian roads in 'Poets Corner' took bomb hits. Tennyson Road was blasted at least twice. In Shakespeare Avenue three women were killed. They had gone to a public shelter on the first night. They stayed home on the second and their house was demolished by a direct hit. In common with other areas, a number of people had trekked from the area south of the river. Mr. Coleman, the warden, had received some assistance from the army on Sunday. That evening he had put some 25 men from the Gloster Regiment into Mary Magdalene Chapel in Holloway. They were to be fire-watchers, to cover for the large number of people who had left their homes. As the raid began to develop, another warden, a Mr. Shearn, was coming down past the chapel:

I was at Holloway on the second night ... The Gloster Regiment were stationed in Mary Magdalene Chapel on Holloway. They were there to help with the water supplies. There were three men in the porch of the church. I was on the opposite side of the road, on patrol coming down from the Bear Flat. You were always told to keep near the wall. I'd just said hello to the men, although I didn't say anything about how dangerous it was, standing out there. It was very clear both nights and you could see the air gunners very low down. I'd just got to the horse trough when I heard a burst of machine-gun fire. I dived for cover near the trough, in the road under the wall. I looked back. Two of the men were on the ground. One had his head shot off. The second was hit in the leg. The third wasn't hit at all. The dead man was a lieutenant. I later had a letter from his mother. I told her that her son had died a hero's death – it was better that way.

Further up the hill stood Beechen Cliff Place. At Number 33, Kathleen Muse was taking cover:

On Sunday my grandmother, daughter and grandson, who had been bombed out on Saturday night from the Lower Bristol Road, were with us. We, my father, mother, sister and myself, got into the Morrison shelter with our dog, a Yorkshire Terrier. So there were seven of us. We stayed there with our fingers in our ears. Then there was a lull and we thought it had stopped. Then there was a whizzing sound; we waited and then it all cascaded down – a ton of bricks. These old houses were well-built and took some blasting. A three-storey house next door came down on us. Mother got the dust from my hair. There was lots of dust from the roof. She was clearing my mouth, ears, hair and made sure it was all okay. The end of the shelter was bent and was almost on mother. We realised we were trapped.

Help was not long in coming. Although the raid had started later than on the first night, it was only a single attack this time. By 02.45 am the raiders had left and the rescue services could go into action.

CHAPTER NINE

Monday

A number of people had survived when their houses had fallen in on top of them; now it was up to the rescue services to try to dig them out. In most cases, survivors were found relatively quickly. In some, it was a race against time. Some people were badly injured and needed urgent medical attention if they were to live. A few died as they were trapped in their houses amidst the debris. Fire broke out in the rubble and they were unable to escape. The other great fear was that no one knew that this house was inhabited or that that one had extra guests that evening. Areas were searched again and again to make sure that everyone was accounted for.

In Holloway, for example, the wardens were soon out trying to locate people. Ron Shearn had an aunt and uncle who owned a shop in Holloway. It took a direct hit. Mr. Shearn's father, who lived there, was found alive, having taken shelter in a cupboard. Next door to the shop, the Full Moon public house was also destroyed. The landlord and two other members of his family were missing. Nearby stood Beechen Cliff Place. The wardens could see that a number of houses along the road had been demolished. With so much destruction, it was hard to know where to dig first, unless some indication was given that there were people still alive under the rubble:

My father shouted for help. Then we all did, in turn. We then heard a man's voice asking if we were alright. We said, yes. He was an old man and couldn't get through to us. He got help and after two and a half hours they had cleared enough debris away for us to be able, just, to crawl out. As we came out, the aircraft came over again and we dived down. We only had our night-clothes on and nothing on our feet. I had a blanket around me. We were taken to a small park and came opposite a woman who was shouting for help, but we couldn't get her out. It was still night and still dark. We watched St. James' Church burning.

(Kathleen Muse)

Everyone helped to dig people out. There were wardens and rescue teams. Mrs. Muse was also helped by a neighbour, a Mr. Pritchard, from a few houses along the road. When Mr. Shearn came to the same road a few hours later there was no one calling out; but once again it was neighbours who helped, this time to pinpoint a trapped person:

Houses came down in Beechen Cliff Place. A Mr. Wilkins was under a table shelter in his house. I saved him as I happened to hear him tapping. There were about seven in his family but they'd all gone to Alexandra Park to sleep out there. It seems he refused to leave and decided to stay in the house that night. I was on patrol, looking for people who needed rescuing. It was well after the bombing and light by then. I was saying, 'Anyone want any water?' People nearby were saying they hadn't seen Mr. Wilkins. I called out to this pile of rubble to see if he was there. I heard tapping and looked down through a little hole. I saw movement. Mr. Wilkins was standing on a stone or a chair in the cellar, about ten feet down. He was still frightened. He said: 'Thank God you've come, Ron.' He didn't need any attention. He was just suffering from shock. I gradually moved the stone and the rubble. I couldn't find any rescue workers. I did it myself. Other neighbours helped, as they were very big stones.

Beechen Cliff Place suffered a great deal of damage but no more than a number of such roads. Mrs. Muse and her family had been rescued; so had Mr. Wilkins. However, when the rescue services had finished there, they had also dug out two people injured and four bodies. Nearby, in Wells Road, was Mr. Shearn's colleague, Mr. Polden. At Number 39 it was known there was a family of four. The father, Mr. Blackburn, was in the RAF and had come home on the Saturday night on leave. He was found with his wife beside him. His coat was around her shoulders. One little girl was taking cover between his legs and his arms were outstretched to protect her. But it was to no avail. All of them were dead, killed when the house collapsed on top of them. A fourth body was found nearby. Next door was another damaged house. Mr. Polden shouted down and this time heard a faint cry that there were nine people trapped under the wreckage. He told them not to worry and eventually, with the aid of soldiers, the Home Guard and a rescue squad, he managed to get them out.

Meanwhile, Kathleen Muse and her family were being given some assistance:

> We went up some steps to a park and after a while we had to move, we were told because of time bombs. It was beginning to get light. Dad went down to the house to get clothes, but couldn't. Then the police and the welfare came and we were taken to St. Mark's Church which was a centre for the bombed-out people. Our names were taken. We all trooped down there. The terrier was alright. We found a thick rope for him. At the school, the vicar came to destroy the dog because he was useless, but we kept him. They fed us there. Mother took us down to town, to Southgate Street where there were drapers' shops. People were helping themselves and I took a scarf and hat. From then on, we were in the hands of the authorities.

What of the authorities? The Germans were busy. Anyone in Britain who cared could tune in on their radio to the New British Broadcasting Station. Supposedly produced by dissident Englishmen, it was, in fact, a rather weak attempt by the Germans to put over their views. No one was fooled. On the Monday it carried a detailed account of the second raid on Bath. A bleak picture was painted. Eyewitnesses compared the city to Coventry. No part had been spared. An hotel, used by the government, had burnt on the first night and been demolished on the second. A nearby shelter collapsed in the same blast and casualties were high. Welfare organisations could not cope with the scale of the disaster. A few personal stories of death completed the broadcast. In fact, as the report was compiled in Germany, there were no eyewitnesses and the whole news item was a fabrication. No such combination of hotel and shelter disaster took place. The more general comments about fires and trekking were obvious ones to make. Another radio broadcast, this time for German home consumption, took a more straightforward line. The idea of reprisal raids was again stressed, although this time the broadcaster also laid great stress on the fact that it was only the rich who could afford to go to Bath. By a series of steps, the announcer claimed that the rich comprised the English ruling classes who, as members of the government, had been responsible for the terror raids on German cultural targets. Once again the lie was repeated that Bath was being attacked because it was a military target, of sorts.

At least, that was the official line. The true state of affairs was shown by a private meeting Goebbels had with Hitler at noon that day. Once again, Hitler was furious at the destruction in Rostock; but he presented Goebbels with some figures that suggested Bath had suffered far more than the German city. Hitler repeated that terror raids must continue against English cultural towns and anywhere not used to being attacked. He talked expansively of a far-reaching plan of such attacks which would surprise the enemy. Terror would be met by terror. The English, he claimed, were the sort of people who had to have their teeth knocked out before they would talk reasonably.

Such forthright language was not intended for publication. The line still went that terror raids on old German cities were being met by revenge raids on British cities that might be old but were also military targets. But only half an hour after Goebbels met Hitler, the Germans made a major propaganda blunder. At the 12.30 pm Foreign Office press conference, a Baron Gustav Braun von Sturm made the first use of the phrase 'Baedeker raid'. The suggestion that the Luftwaffe would now attack every city emphasised in the famous series of guidebooks, was one eagerly revived by the British press as another example of German barbarity. The admission that the Germans were bombing British cultural targets was such a useful one that it was not long before the phrase was being ascribed to everyone in the German High Command, Hitler included.

It was a minor victory for the British. It meant very little to those in Bath. Once again, the local authorities were faced by a bewildering series of problems. There were 35 major fires. Of these, there were serious ones at the Royal Crescent, Stothert & Pitt and the Assembly Rooms. Casualties were numerous. Reinforcements were flooding in but these were hampered by the transport situation. The two main railway lines were severely restricted. A number of damaged bridge parapets and the presence of unexploded bombs kept traffic to a minimum. When a number of the Sadler's Wells company attempted to leave the city they found it impossible to move from Green Park station. Bath Spa was also damaged and they had to walk out to Batheaston before they could get a train back to London. The roads were similarly dislocated. Two major roads, Wells Road and Lower Bristol Road, were blocked. Unexploded bombs cut off others. Rescue squads and a large contingent from the Welsh Guards were busy making ways through. The local newspaper carried the optimistic note that bus services were normal in the sense that all routes were being served, however infrequently.

The basic services were also in some disarray. The gas mains were in such a mess that strict instructions were given to keep all gas taps off. Water was available, except in the Lansdown area, but should be boiled. Food was in plentiful supply as the emergency teams, such as the Queen's Messengers and YMCA vehicles, had turned out again. Mobile canteens took food and drink to various places, the Pump Room, for example, and even to trekkers outside the city. The rest centres also provided tea and biscuits for the distressed, and hot meals, prepared at St. Martin's hospital. Some places went through their food supplies rather quickly because of over-generous helpings. But the Ministry of Food replaced the stocks very quickly. A number of bakeries had been destroyed. Very few shops were open, but there was no shortage of food.

London was already sending down investigators to see how Bath was coping under the strain. One who arrived on Monday went to the Civil Defence Headquarters at the Foresters Arms and felt that things were chaotic there. In fact, the situation was largely under control as later investigators were to comment. Most of the services were working as well as could be expected, although many of the local personnel were tiring, having been on duty continuously for the two nights. At least one member of the Home Guard had been on duty since 11.15 pm on Saturday night. Most wardens were on duty continually until Monday morning. Herbert Bath, the fireman, worked just as long. A number of the ambulance drivers, Don Tuddenham for example, only went home for a few hours for a meal or a change of clothes and then went back on duty. The doctors were even fewer in number and, therefore, even more in demand. Some 100 cases were treated at the RUH until the staff were completely exhausted, and the hospital was full. Some had to be sent to Gloucester Hospital. St. Martin's dealt with twice as many casualties, making room by evacuating more soldier patients. On Monday, Dr. Kohn and his team were working without a stop. The Bristol Minister of Health rang again, offering a relief team of doctors. They arrived that afternoon to take over, but even so, Dr. Kohn and his men were still at the hospital at 11.00 pm, checking the progress of the patients that they had already operated upon.

Only the mortuary service was, temporarily, overwhelmed. A number of the mortuaries had suffered damage. St. Peter's could not do work at night because of damage to its roof. St. James' had been burned out. On Monday morning the bodies in the crypt had to be moved to the nearby Weymouth House School. This was not a pleasant job, wading around in the water-logged crypt, picking up corpses. Robert Smith, the ambulance driver, found they had to knock down a brick wall in front of the school door before they could get the bodies in. The wall was a protection against blast. The mortuary staff worked long hours to cope with the large number of bodies. On the first night they turned in for 19 hours duty and 12 on the next night and still they could not cope. Not only did the bodies have to be prepared for burial, there was also the all-important question of identification. If a body was brought out from a known address and was recognised by a warden or neighbour, or if it had some written form of identification on it, then a label would be attached to it. Relatives could come along to identify a corpse and if they claimed the body, it could be removed for private burial. After the first night of the raids there were a large number of such demands. Undertakers were inundated with requests for private burials. Without notice to the council, some removed their staff from the mortuaries to meet these demands, leaving even fewer skilled men to deal with the bodies. Many were not identified immediately or could not be. Most were identified within a few days and most relatives were satisfied with the idea of a council burial. A communal grave had been dug at Haycombe Cemetery on Sunday, but already it was realised it would not be large enough. Unfortunately, the situation was complicated by the fact that there was an unexploded bomb at the entrance to the cemetery, hampering further work.

It was estimated that there might be 175 dead. The final toll was double that and more, but while many were still buried in the ruins of their houses, any figure could only be approximate. The sooner one was rescued, the better one's chances of survival. Muriel Gough and her family had already been trapped for some seven hours:

> It wasn't until 8.00 am, a long time ... when the neighbours came down and found we weren't there. My mother had told them of the Morrison. They went to the police but they said they needed proof that we were alive before they started to dig, as there were too many calls. We reckoned that we were trapped for seven or eight hours, although it felt like eighty hours or eighty days. We thought we heard people calling out on top. My father said that he would count to three and we'd all yell. We did this. Afterwards they said it sounded like one little child. The neighbours

had gone straight to the police and got a twenty-man team there. They felt they knew where the shelter was. They made a passageway down. My father was on top and got out. A lady with us was pregnant and she was got out. Mr. Russell, with us, was across us and pinning my leg down. A doctor came down and gave him an injection. He asked if there was anything I needed as he had to go to cut the wire ... he said he had to go to the house opposite as he'd heard cries for help. They had no cellars there, but one man was trapped as the front of the house had come down with our bomb. He was trapped on the sofa. They found him, but once they'd got him out, he died. They came back with secateurs and cut the wire. Mr. Russell's leg was just bruised. I was alright, if rather numb. They carried us out across the rubble.

With only a limited number of rescue squads available, not all blitzed sites could be searched at once. At Kingsmead Terrace, one squad had spent a number of hours searching and sifting through the rubble. They had found nothing. That Monday evening a Mr. Cutting arrived home on compassionate leave from the RAF to find that his parents' home in the Terrace was completely destroyed. Along with his brother, also on leave, Mr. Cutting probed the piles of wreckage until at last he heard a voice crying from somewhere underneath. He tunnelled down and called out. A weak voice replied, 'It's Ivor. Raymond is here with me. He is alright. Mum and dad are with us but they are dead.' Mr. Cutting, having proved that there were people alive and trapped at the site, went off and got a rescue team. Eventually they managed to release Mr. Cutting's younger brother, Ivor, and his nephew Raymond; but both parents and four other members of the family were dead. The two survivors had been trapped under the stairs with the bodies of their relatives for more than a day.

One of the main rescue incidents was at the Regina Hotel. The staff and those guests who had gone to the basement shelter were led out by wardens. Within the hotel, a number of lives had been saved as well. One member of the Home Guard, Mr. Leslie, had been active even when the raid was still on. He had worked his way down through the rubble, through a small hole to the basement. There, a woman had been trapped by falling masonry. Mr. Leslie supported her, for a number of hours, until rescue squads could get to her. Fires nearby threatened both their lives and at times Mr. Leslie had to be doused with water to prevent his clothes catching fire. As the day wore on, more people were found in the remains of the collapsed half of the hotel. Lady King was recovered and taken to hospital. She died there next day. On Monday, though, it was largely a case of trying to work out who had been there in the first place. A local newspaper carried a report that the Reverend Woodmansey was believed to have been standing outside the Regina when the bomb fell. As yet, no trace of him had been found. Opposite the hotel, the Assembly Rooms were still burning for most of Monday. A few rooms survived intact but the main part was gutted by fire. One London investigator found firemen damping down the fire while exhibitions of gowns still stood, forlornly, nearby. A sedan chair, relatively undamaged, sat amidst the ruins. This most famous architectural loss in the raids soon attracted attention. One woman who trekked out on Monday night temporarily lost track of her young brother. He had disappeared with a number of friends to go up and look at the smoking remains of the Assembly Rooms before leaving Bath for the night.

Few people, except for the young, made a conscious effort to go and look at the famous sites that had been destroyed. Trekkers had returned to the city on Monday morning, although few had the problem that Jill Clayton's mother faced. Mother and daughter had spent the night at an army camp outside the city:

> During the night my mother appeared to be in pain as she kept moving about and moaning. In the morning, my father came in the car to pick us up. He was in a reserved occupation, doing haulage work for the army, RAF and the

like. He took us back into Bath but it was very hard as there were bomb craters in many of the roads. We finally got through Oldfield Park and came up towards Wells Road. I felt car sick, so we stopped and I was sick in someone's garden. We went on to Bear Flat and up to Bloomfield Road. Then my mother remembered she had left her leather coat behind on a wall and wanted to go back for it – clothes were very expensive and rare then. My father said we ought to get her to hospital. We went back for the coat after a quarrel! We got home again and my mother was found to have acute appendicitis and she went to hospital.

Many stuck to routine and, as far as possible, tried to get to work. One house help turned up as usual after spending two nights crouching in a public shelter in Oldfield Park. Miss Meredith had spent Sunday night at the Methodist chapel in Corston. Having gone home first, she set out somewhat later than usual for her office in the city. There were no buses. At the office everything was in a state of confusion. In a top room one of the women, clad in trousers, was trying to sweep some of the mess. Frank Selwyn had an even livelier walk to work:

On Monday morning I got up to go to work at the Technical College. I was in the electrical engineering division. I started to walk from Newbridge. I got to the gasworks. Nobody stopped me. I saw something standing about three feet above the ground. It was an unexploded bomb in the road with its tail sticking out. The area was cordoned off, but somehow I got through, I don't know how. Traffic was diverted and they removed it fairly quickly. I nipped off pretty smartly – it was an unexpected thing.

Perhaps it was the one that William Smith had come into contact with:

On the Upper Bristol Road, in the middle of the road, was an unexploded bomb. On top of it was a beer barrel, to show where the bomb was, but no one paid any notice to it, especially as the tail of my ambulance smashed the barrel. We had to make detours but we got a bit blasé about unexploded bombs.

Many people were unable to work that day. Mark Whiteley's father was an engineer working on gun mountings at Stothert & Pitt's. He was off work for a number of days as a series of bombs had hit the works. School children were also starting a new week. Many felt that whatever had happened, they must go to school as usual:

> I was in the first year of the City of Bath Girls' School. We couldn't stay away when we were ill, so we went as usual. We were too frightened not to. We got down to Moorland Road but couldn't get around because of the hosepipes and fires. Nor could we get around Lower Oldfield Park. We went up Junction Road and eventually got to school. When we got there we were told to go home and wait until it said in the paper. We went round looking for shrapnel and bullet cases. Everyone was doing that. You polished them and put them on your mantelpiece.
>
> (Kathleen Stainer)

Walter Sweetenham was a pupil at the City of Bath Boys' School. His father worked for the Admiralty in Bath and on Monday the two set off from their home in Keynsham:

> On Monday morning I went in with my father in the car. There was much glass everywhere but we didn't get a puncture. The army was on point duty on the Upper Bristol Road and directed us around the debris. There was debris everywhere. There had been attempts to push it to one side. Soldiers with rifles on their backs were directing the traffic. We weren't asked why we were coming into Bath. We reached the centre and I eventually got to school. We were heading for the Empire Hotel. My father dropped me

and I walked. I don't recall any real difficulty in getting to school. There were huge chunks of stone in the Avenues, which you had to get around, and rescue squads looking for survivors. There didn't seem to be a lot of people around. Bear Flat and Holloway were badly hit. The City of Bath Boys' School had had bombs that landed near. One landed in the cricket pitch and caused a fire in the history room and the senior chemistry lab. But staff and pupil fire-watchers had put the fire out with fire appliances. One of the playgrounds had a field kitchen for cooking and this was used immediately. The assembly hall was a rest centre and serving one hot meal a day at a very low price. You might get mince, potatoes and a cup of tea, all for 6d (2½p). The place wasn't used as a school. There were a number of pupils there but we felt it was an invasion from outside. There was an army detachment billeted there, in the cloakroom, I think. We helped to clear up the debris. Some of my colleagues lost their homes. One was the only survivor of his family as the house fell down on them. We treated it as a matter of fact. We talked about people being killed. There were quite a few at school chatting about it ... I don't know if anyone from school was killed although I assume it would be likely. No one I knew particularly well in my own year was killed.

Rumours of deaths and people missing were soon flying around. The fact that Bath had been bombed had been announced on the radio; many friends and relatives elsewhere had a natural worry for those in the city. With so much debris and such poor communications, a flood of visitors was the last thing that was needed. The Ministry of Information made a public announcement asking the public to refrain, at present, from travelling to and from Bath. Even so, some people had to make a journey out of desperation. A Mr. and Mrs. Cooper had been living in Bath for a year before the raids. The husband had been on fire-watching duty on the first night. After the first raid he had called at his wife's lodgings and had a chat with his wife and her friends. Then the second raid began; Mr. Cooper returned to duty and was killed. Mrs. Cooper sent a telegram to her sister, Mrs. Taylor, who lived with her daughter, Joan, in Staines. Mrs. Taylor received this message at 8.00 am on the Monday. Just over an hour later, she set off with her daughter, by car, to Bath. When they arrived, Mrs. Taylor helped her bereaved sister to pack so that they could all go back to Staines that very night. Meanwhile, Joan Taylor went into the city to try to find Mr. Cooper's body. Lists of named bodies were posted in a number of prominent positions around Bath. Joan went to the Guildhall first and found a list that said that Mr. Cooper had been taken to the crypt of St. James'. However, as an outsider, she had no idea of the situation there. When Joan got to the church she saw it had been badly damaged. It was still smouldering and several hoses were still being played on it. A police constable nearby told her that it would be impossible to identify any body. The ink on the identifying labels had run, after being immersed in water. Furthermore, the crypt was not only flooded, but there was also danger of structural collapse. Joan Taylor returned to the Guildhall to try to find further details but the situation was confused there, and no one could tell her where the bodies would be taken to from the crypt. Eventually the three women had to give up and went to Staines for the night.

Another person with worries was Grace Horler:

At the time we were living in Tenby, Pembrokeshire, where my husband was stationed with a battalion of Royal Marines. The first raid was on a Saturday night and the following morning the radio said: 'Last night there was a heavy raid on a town in Somerset.' They were censored so no name was given. I said: 'Poor Bristol again, I expect.' Later news said it was Bath. My concern was for my elderly mother living at 4 Eastbourne Avenue, Claremont Road, and a friend who lived with her. The following Monday morning I received a letter from her saying she was alright. However, on the Sunday night there was another raid so the letter gave me no hope. Everyone said: 'The police will tell you if she is dead.' There were few 'phones then; we relied on letters.

Mrs. Horler had to just sit and wait for a further message. One other person, who did act immediately, was Henry Gough, then not yet married to his future wife. He was in the army, stationed at Wimborne, and heard on the radio on the Monday that Bath had been bombed. He knew nothing of the state of Muriel Gough or of his own family but he was granted a 72 hour leave pass. At once he set off by train to Bath.

Many people in Bath needed some assistance; Florence Delve in particular:

I spent three nights sleeping with the babies in a horse's shed in Kingswood Gardens, at the top of Kingswood School, at the top of the allotments. I just sat there with my two babies. One neighbour at the bottom of the hill did come to the allotments on Monday afternoon with a cup of tea. She said I could come to her house for an hour's rest. But I needed a bed to sleep in. That's all I can remember in the way of offers. Everyone was so busy seeing for themselves.

Many had little real idea of what they should be doing. A second night of raids had made more homeless. Most were agitated and shocked to a greater or lesser degree. A London investigator who toured the city went to such bombed sites as the Scala shelter, Elm Grove Terrace and Holloway. Everywhere he found the same conditions. Most people he talked to showed signs of severe strain. They were nervous and agitated. They tended to repeat the same story over and over again. Most people were detached from their normal routine and had not settled into a new one. Some just wandered around. The streets were full of people with nothing particular to do. They walked aimlessly in the centre of the city even though few shops were open. Some roads were full of rubble. There were piles of glass everywhere. Fires were still burning with clouds of dense, acrid smoke. Dust shrouded everything and made everyone thirsty. Crowds gathered around the various assistance bureaux. In parks and sites groups of homeless people could be seen. Some were sheltering in tents made from their bedclothes. In one park a family had gathered together all their surviving possessions: a chest of drawers, bedding, a few suitcases of clothes, a pram and a bird in a cage. One small boy was dressed only in his pyjamas and an overcoat. One woman remembers seeing people in the streets with prams, carts and other modes of transport filled with the odd possession. Two children walked through the city pushing a tin bath containing just a broken doll.

For one girl, the worst sight was the large number of people leaving the city. Unending streams poured from the town. Many were absolutely silent. They appeared stunned and incapable, at times, of realising where they were. Some carried bundles or pushed prams containing all they had left. A second, consecutive night of raids proved the final straw for many people. Once again the local authorities gave some assistance and provided extra buses, although there were never quite enough. Large queues built up at the Parade Gardens. A Mrs. Warne saw a sea of people there. There were many queues but no bus schedules. With no visible organisation, people were getting on to any bus and just going anywhere. Some had their own transport. Mrs. Smith, who had spent the night in the railway tunnel, returned home to find that only the front ceiling had come down although there was other, lesser damage as well. With a number of other families and in a couple of cars, Mrs. Smith drove out of the city and into the fields where the whole party spent a very cold night.

It is impossible to say how many trekked out on the second night; but it was certainly far more than on the Sunday evening. As one woman put it, after the second night, people were just shattered. Mrs. Gough and her family were evacuated to Dunkerton where they were split up. The men were sent to the Baptist chapel and the women to the Sunday school. Kathleen Muse went to relatives in Swainswick. A third bomb victim, Eric Davies, went even further:

> On the third night I had 5/- (25p) to get to near Stroud. We got to Stonehouse and then had no money. We were like gypsies. My wife had some nappies given to her and a coat three times as big as her. We had 6d (2½p) left and my wife said I should use it for a pint. The landlord of the pub asked if we were from Bath. I said we were, but were stuck. I wasn't going to beg. He called a man out and said he had a car. The man drove us to Stroud. Another person then drove us to my sister.

Edward and Winifred Hurford walked out to Hampton Rocks with hundreds of others although they didn't sleep because it was so cold. Mrs. Potter and her family also left:

> After the two terrible nights of the Bath Blitz, which I remember only as being terribly noisy, we packed a case and our parents took us up to Hampton Rocks. Crowds of people were flocking there for the night. We left our old grandma at home as, being stone deaf and bedridden, she didn't even know there was a war on! We spent the night together huddled on Hampton Rocks.

Some had, originally, no intention of leaving, but later changed their minds:

> People started collecting their belongings and leaving until it was eventually just three of our families that would be left in the street. Therefore, we packed up our bedding, strapped it on our backs, and walked up past Englishcombe and settled down in the rows along the lane, on the grass verge at the side. It was moonlight and we had to keep our faces covered in case the German bombers saw us and machine-gunned us. We were laid out with our eiderdowns with us. There must have been dozens of us there ... we tied the stuff on our backs and just walked out to Englishcombe.

We were wearing warm clothes, gloves and a hat. It must have been cold but I can't remember. Anyway, I slept. A lot of people went to village halls. We just followed the others in our street.

(Kathleen Stainer)

In Shakespeare Avenue, more and more people left until it seemed that Mr. and Mrs. Horsell were the only people left there. One girl felt it strange that in so many houses there were so few people. When Henry Gough finally got back to Bath, he too found the city deserted:

It was dark when the train ran into Bathampton station, and I was obliged to disembark as the railway lines to Bath station were under repair. I walked into Bath from Bath-ampton and did not meet a human being. St. James' Church had been badly hit and as I turned the corner into Kingston Road I saw Number 2 had had a direct hit. I had no means of knowing whether the occupants were dead or alive. I journeyed on to my own home in Victoria Terrace, Oldfield Park, and here the whole of Victoria Road was down, the street shelters being covered in rubble. My own home was very badly damaged ... Later I was told by a friend that my wife's family were alive and were at Longfellow Avenue with Mr. and Mrs. Frank Blake.

Bath was virtually deserted on the Monday night. One more incendiary attack, with fewer people there to put the fires out, might have devastated the city. However many Civil Defence personnel and active defenders were available, without householders to back them up, they could do little to stem a large number of fires. At Colerne and Charmy Down the local squadrons were looking forward to a more successful third night of interceptions. For the first time, Bath also had its own anti-aircraft defences. Six mobile guns were rushed to the hills around the city. One stood on Lansdown. Other mobile guns were taken to other likely targets such as Canterbury and

Penzance. In fact, the guesses were all wrong. On the night of April 27th, the Germans struck at Norwich. The air raids on Bath were over.

CHAPTER TEN

The First Week

The trekkers who returned home on Tuesday morning had, by and large, spent a cold and often miserable night under the stars. Some had been lucky enough to stay with friends and relations. A number had slept in church halls and other public buildings. Although the city had not been blitzed again, this gave little comfort. The Germans had a habit of returning to previously bombed cities. Exeter, the first target in this series of raids, was also bombed a number of weeks after, on May 4th. This proved the most destructive raid of all on that city. A radio broadcast, mentioning the fact that the centre of Bath and the Abbey had not been hit, caused further alarm. If the Germans were listening in, then they might come back to finish the job. Fear of another raid was best illustrated by an incident which occurred on the Tuesday afternoon. A lone German aircraft flew over the city, causing the air raid sirens to be sounded again. There was a general rush for the shelters. Some people, fearing it was another major attack, became greatly agitated. Henry Gough was looking around the ruins of his wife's house to see if he could salvage anything when the warning sounded. Along with a great number of others, he went to the shelter in the Parade Gardens. The 'all clear' sounded only a quarter of an hour later when it was realised that there was only one aircraft on a reconnaissance mission. This was still enough to upset many, as Mr. Tuddenham admitted:

We were all scared when the reconnaissance plane came over. A man broke down and cried. We all could have. There were no brave men.

87 Squadron sent up two patrols in an attempt to intercept the intruder, but they failed to make contact. One of the photos taken by the German aircraft was published a few months later in the official magazine of Luftflotte III, the air fleet responsible for the bombing of Bath. Under the title 'Bath after the German reprisal raid' a photo-map of the west of

the city was reproduced with areas of greatest damage drawn around, and the more noticeable single bombs ringed. The most striking areas were those that had already been partially cleared, which showed up as light coloured; areas such as Roseberry Road, Elm Grove Terrace and the Regina Hotel. One such area in Avon Street had not been bombed though; it was a slum area, demolished by the council before the war. Nor, despite German claims, had most of the Royal Crescent and the Circus been badly damaged in the raids.

It was an obvious fear that a reconnaissance aircraft was only flying overhead to find out which areas of the city still needed to be bombed. The nightly exodus of trekkers continued. The queues for buses at the Parade Gardens became a regular feature. Some people created whole new routines:

My sister-in-law had relatives at Chilcompton and in view of the fact that my mother had been ill, and sundry other considerations, it was decided that mother and I and her mother and sister should travel out there each evening when we three girls had finished work. We were kindly accommodated by two lots of relatives for the night, then came back to Bath again in the morning. This we did for a week. We were able to travel thus as fortunately the Midland Railway was undamaged but the GWR was unusable.

(Miss Meredith)

There were so many wrecked homes in Bath and so many homeless people that the council had to try any means to accommodate them. The town clerk went so far as to request that Bath be designated an evacuation area. But the Regional officer refused, saying that there were vacant spaces in the city. Many rooms were supposed to have been left unoccupied by the rich who, since the bombing, had left the city. The council encouraged women, children and the old to leave the city. Extra petrol coupons were available from the Guildhall for those with cars who wished to evacuate their families. The homeless who packed the rest centres were moved out to surrounding areas. As many as possible were put in touch with friends and relatives. On Wednesday, 160 homeless people were evacuated to Trowbridge where they slept in such places as church halls and even club skittle alleys. Others went to Lacock, south Somerset and west Wiltshire. The only major problem was that there were a number of old people without friends or relations to help them. Most were eventually sent to suitable hostels in Bristol and elsewhere. It was claimed that by Wednesday evening every homeless person in Bath had been found a billet, but some were rather better than others. At least one man spent some weeks sleeping rough in a barn. Florence Delve also had to take matters into her own hands:

By Wednesday I was just about round the bend. All my senses were going. I decided to go to my mother. We walked from Bath to Bristol. We just trudged it to Bristol Temple Meads with the two babies. I can't remember that journey. I feel that I didn't know what was going on. I remember my husband saying he had to get me to my mother. I said I didn't want to bother her. I don't remember the bit from Bristol to my mother in Tonypandy. I just remember walking in. But when we got to her, she said I'd gone white. I hadn't, but I was covered in dust and plaster. I hadn't had a wash. My husband had to go back to Stothert & Pitt's.

Others were busy trying to make their homes habitable. By Wednesday there were nearly 2,000 men working on basic house repairs. Householders were asked to remove debris from their houses and deposit it in their front gardens. The council would arrange for it to be picked up later. Plaster, wooden laths and in particular, glass, were swept out of many homes. People were encouraged to go to various depots to pick up free materials for simple jobs. Felt and various types of transparent material were available along with nails and lathes for boarding up broken windows. The next greatest worry was the state of many roofs. Fred Short was involved in such repairs:

The builders were organised. They made good what damage they could repair; for example they put linen over the windows and covered the roofs with tarpaulins, etc. ... We continued with rescue work, identification and the setting up of what shelter we could, for the homeless, which involved making something safe. For example, we would make damaged houses as safe as possible for their owners who were often sheltering in the communal shelters.

Relatively few houses had suffered severe structural damage, but slates off the roof, ceilings down, windows and doors blown out and dust and dirt everywhere were bad enough. Most homes lost cherished personal possessions, such as china shattered by near misses, as well. Nor was all damage immediately obvious as Sam Hayward, the warden, discovered:

I went next door to clear out the glass but all the old dear said was: 'Look what that Hitler has done to me. If I could get my hands on him!' We lost our windows. There was also dust and dirt. All the ceilings were down, except for the front room one. It was very dry and cold, with a bitterly cold wind. After the raids we had a fellow in to do repairs. He said the wall on the right of the hall was on the point of collapsing. They asked if I would pay if I couldn't get anything for war damages. My wife came home to find the wall down. It was later paid for out of the war damages fund. It was a wonder the wall hadn't collapsed before.

Rose Miller spent some time in hospital before being allowed home. When she returned to her house it was to find that in some ways it was lucky she had gone to West Twerton School:

Eventually when I got home, my brother was there on leave. We had some damage. The front door was blown in. A shell had gone through the wardrobe. It had come through the window and the glass of the wardrobe. The shell was inside a dress in the wardrobe. It lifted the dress off of the hanger. This had been just after I left. It had been so hot that it burnt the dress. Shrapnel knocked off a Harpic tin in the bathroom. All the powder in the room went round and burnt the floor. The shrapnel went through the landing and into the one boy's bedroom. He'd never stay at home which was good for him as he'd have been killed. His bedding was slit as if someone had been through it with a knife.

Sam Hayward found not only that his house was a mess, but also that eating was a problem. Tea was provided by mobile canteens. After the first couple of days following the raids, the demand for meals at the emergency canteens increased greatly. People could put up with a lack of gas and water for only a short while. On Tuesday, 5,000 people were served; by Friday 30,000 meals were being provided each day. New centres opened daily. The Pump Room served meals such as roast beef along with suet pudding for 1/- (5p). The food was cooked in Bristol and brought to Bath in vacuum containers. The canteen was run by staff and students from the local Domestic Science college. There were six similar canteens. There were also a large number of emergency feeding centres giving hot food to the homeless, and many more mobile canteens run by half a dozen different voluntary organisations: the YMCA, Queen's Messengers, Ministry of Food, amongst others. Supply almost kept up with demand. A number of school girls helped provide food, peeling potatoes and brewing up tea. Meals became one continual blur with breakfast running into lunch and lunch into tea; although some people were still too shocked at times to know what meal they were eating. Washing up posed another problem when water was limited and often cold. Walter Sweetenham at the City of Bath Boys' School, gave some help:

For a week there was no real school, but we were encouraged to go back if we could. There were quite a number of people there for meals. The electricity had failed and many were without gas. I think it was the WVS working up there. We sometimes helped with the meals. We were detailed to collect plates and cups. Some of my colleagues peeled potatoes. We got our own meals there as well. Some people were quite shocked. There were usually one or two men there from the National Benefit Office who would give small sums of money if you were bombed out. They also gave advice. One didn't really appreciate the situation – that people had nothing.

Static tanks of drinking water were set up in some places. Milk was available from any milkman, but one had to bring one's own container. To help morale, a number of rarely seen commodities made an appearance. Fry's sent in chocolate. Whisky, previously only available on the black market, turned up as well. Most shops stayed shut for the week although some did a little trading from temporary stalls or the backs of their buildings. Those who did venture into the centre of the city found that much had changed. Kingsmead Street and part of New King Street were closed off for some time. There were a number of unexploded bombs in some areas, but Kingsmead Street was so badly hit that it was dangerous to walk down. The street was roped off with placards at either end. People were held back, crying, from rubble that was still smoking. Soldiers were on patrol in the street itself. Anne Marks wanted to see what had happened to her school friends there. Jill Clayton also went looking for her friends:

My father's secretary's mother suggested I go and see my friends but there was no one there. They had gone for at least a week. The Anderson shelter opposite was completely destroyed. It was a house shelter that held about ten people. We never used shelters; in this case it was just as well.

It was not just the destruction of houses that drew people's attention. It was also the strange sight of personal possessions exposed to public view. Bernard Humphries likened the blitzed terraces to rows of teeth with gaps. Some had been sliced through and perched above the streets, stranded pieces of furniture looking as if they were in doll's houses. Miss Meredith saw a piano, which belonged to a relative, standing in the middle of the road at Second Avenue. One girl, who helped to serve meals, had felt guilty because she had come through the raids without any real hardship:

> Everyone was amazingly cheerful, but then everyone had something to do and there was little time to think or ponder over what had happened. I can remember feeling very guilty and ashamed, although I was most thankful too, at having to reply to many questions of those less fortunate: 'No, not even a pane of glass!'
>
> I received many shocks at that time, some pleasant and others infinitely less so, but the most profound of all occurred some time later. It was raining fairly hard and I was walking under an umbrella, my gaze fixed steadily on the ground, thinking as I had often done before, of how cosy it must be in those houses on either side of me, and how I too would soon be by the fireside reading a book. Quite suddenly I looked up – why I don't know – and saw beside me only gaunt blackened shells of houses, outlined against the sky and the water dripping slowly and horribly from the charred timbers. Never since then have I felt complacent or even so secure ...

The photographs of the damage tend to show isolated piles of rubble on the site of what was once a house. Most of these photos were taken days after the raids, and do not show the initial full devastation and confusion. Fred Short spent the first few days organising his men and trying to make pathways through the piles of debris, as there was no time, as yet, to clear them away. Bomb craters in the road had to be filled in with all the surrounding debris, stonework, tiles and anything else that was handy. Houses that had been destroyed had their rubble tidied up and just thrown back onto the wrecked site. There was so much debris around that it had to be got rid of wherever possible. One bomb had fallen in St. James' cemetery. Mr. Short got one of his men to stand at the entrance to the cemetery to flag down passing lorries so they could empty their debris into the crater there. The wreckage could present its own shocks. Tony Self, then a child, was walking around town with his family:

> At the corner of the Francis Hotel I saw an arm sticking out. I was told it was a doll, but I didn't believe it. I was just fascinated and wanted to get nearer.

While most people in Bath were trying to get back to normal, the workers continued to look through the rubble for missing persons. Despite their best efforts, the wardens could never keep track of everyone; who was exactly where on the nights of the raids, especially at a busy weekend. The big Georgian houses consisting of a number of separate flats could hold a large number of people. Many had moved about during the lull on Saturday night. A number of the hotels had been particularly lax in providing the wardens with up-to-date lists of their guests. In most cases, therefore, all that could be done was a patient, stone by stone search through the rubble until all casualties or bodies had been found. As the days passed, it became obvious that the chances of finding people alive were rapidly diminishing. However, the occasional miraculous survival story tended to encourage those whose relatives were still missing. Over 100 rescue squads, numerous soldiers and other members of the armed forces were engaged in such work but, even so, they could not be everywhere at once. At small sites that had already been explored by rescue squads and where it was felt no one could be alive, surviving members of the family might still be poking through the wreckage, looking for any sign of their relatives.

All the part time members of the local rescue squads worked full time for a number of weeks. The Regional headquarters sent a large number of reinforcements on the first few days, although after that they were reluctant to send many more. Albert Davis was involved at a number of sites:

The rescue party leader was in charge of the site and his duties were to locate casualties and then search the house for others. If we needed help, we called for a policeman via the despatch riders who would look after the corpses until the mortuary vans came to pick them up. To help identify the corpses, I wrote labels with the name and location and time of incident and stuck them on the bodies. We studied houses and learnt their construction from local wardens to find where the stairs were so that if the place was bombed, we could dig to them. We learnt everything by practice. In Bath we had an extra hazard. The houses were full of cellars. Many people went into them and had to look out as bombs fell and broke the water mains and flooded cellars, I was up to my knees in water in one cellar. There was also the problem of ordinary gas. We had remote-control breathing apparatus, a mask on the face and tube leading to fresh air.

At most incidents the rescue party leader had a team of soldiers or other unskilled workers that he could guide and direct as he saw fit. Henry Hamlin had to spend most of his time in the office directing operations, but was called out early on for one particular case:

One time I was asked to come to Northampton Street. I was taken on a motorbike by a despatch rider. When I arrived, I first told the squad to get the dead off the road and under cover: we had to keep morale up. The problem was of an elderly man in the basement. There was a beam across the top of his legs and he was leaning over it. My colleague asked how could we get him out? I said to loop a rope around his ankles and pull him out that way. My friend asked whether that wouldn't cause the rest of the roof to fall in if he was moved. I said he couldn't be holding it all up by himself. Anyway, we got him out my way. It didn't matter really, he was obviously dead. You could tell by the way his head was resting on his chest.

It was even more difficult to get to trapped people who were still alive. Dr. Astley-Weston knew of one such casualty who was trapped under rubble and badly needed morphia. The rescue parties could not get her out immediately. An elderly doctor worked at the nearby first aid post along with a woman. This woman was small enough to be lowered down through a hole in the rubble to the injured person. She took a syringe filled with morphia and was able to administer an injection. Another medical officer managed to crawl into a demolished house to give injections to a trapped woman but the woman died soon after. The medical officer himself suffered some degree of shock after this incident.

In Holloway Ron Shearn's father had already been rescued from the shop next door to the Full Moon. A few days later, rescue squads arrived to search the ruins of the pub itself. It was hoped that someone might have survived if they had taken shelter in the cellar. A squad from Bristol had brought along some sound detectors which they applied to the rubble. Eventually, they heard the sound of someone tapping faintly. Digging down, they finally found the landlord of the pub, Mr. William Small, alive and well. Two members of his family were found dead, however, in the same building. In New King Street a Mr. Swatton had been digging in the ruins of his house. He found the body of one of his daughters on Tuesday, April 28th. It was her birthday. Other houses in the same street had been demolished but the sheer size of them meant that bodies were being dug out for days afterwards. The same went for the Paragon where Dr. Middlemas' house was only one of a number in a row that had been destroyed. This had turned into a major incident. Mrs. Horsell went there on Tuesday with a doctor, as casualties had been found still alive. One woman was trapped there and while workers were trying to get her out they passed tea to her via a can and a length of rubber tubing. That evening, William Smith helped to get out one woman:

It was the 'Is this a stunt?' lady. We got her out from the Paragon on Tuesday night, from Dr. Middlemas' house. She was carried out and had a military escort to take her to the hospital. She had been buried since Saturday.

The woman was one who received great prominence in a booklet published soon after the raids. An elderly lady, she was reported as having been put into an ambulance after being rescued, when she suddenly sat up and asked the attendant:

Tell me, young man – was this a real raid or just one of your practice stunts?

Robert Smith, also an ambulance driver, had memories of the same person:

At the Paragon, Dr. Middlemas of the Snow Hill post was reported missing. The rescue men dug into the debris and first found the body of a man. The ceiling had come down diagonally and the lady was in the void, by a gas cooker. The rescue workers said there was a casualty there who was still alive. I had just got back to the depot in the ambulance, having just collected a lot of pork pies. Two of us went down to the Paragon and Dr. Weston gave her an injection. She asked for her handbag, then her glasses, then her false teeth so she could eat. We got her into the ambulance and she asked whether this was a real raid. We got her to hospital, but I think she died on Friday.

Vic Penny also helped to get one person out from the Paragon. While digging through the rubble he could still hear a voice calling out. The woman died soon after he reached her. The rescuers dug down further and further into the rubble, but it was not until Wednesday that Dr. Mary Middlemas' body was found. Wearing her fur coat and tin helmet, it was obvious that she had been in the act of going back on duty when the bomb had fallen. Lying nearby were the bodies of her two sisters, Elsie who lived with her, and Jean who had been on a short visit to Bath. A short time later, two other bodies were discovered. They were later identified as Dr. Middlemas' two maids, Freda Baker and Edna Hawkins. It appeared they had survived the bombing, but had been trapped when the remains of the building had caught fire. Unable to escape, they had been burned to death. Miss Hawkins could only be identified, by her father, by the watch that she wore. Miraculously, one more person was found alive at the Paragon. At 9.00 pm on Wednesday, rescue workers heard the faint sound of tapping under the rubble. They called out: 'Is anyone there?' and heard a young girl call back. Pulling aside the stones and other wreckage, the men uncovered a cupboard in which they found a young girl sitting alone, clutching a spoon. Having taken shelter in the cupboard when the house collapsed, she had felt around and found the spoon. She had tapped it against the walls of the cupboard until she had finally heard the sound of a pick and shovel. She had been buried for well over three days when they finally dug her out on that Wednesday evening. Unknown to all, she was the last person to be brought out alive from the ruins in Bath.

The hunt for bodies went on. On Saturday, May 2nd, a number of sites yielded up their dead. A bomb had fallen in Howells Court, a cul-de-sac in the south of the city. One family there had vacated the city, another had taken cover in a Morrison shelter. The Rattray family had been caught by the blast, and on that Saturday the bodies of nine members of the one family were discovered. In the Kingsmead area, individuals were still sifting through the rubble of their houses. A Private Davis had moved down to Bath with his family from London only the year before. They lived in a top flat in 32 Kingsmead Street. One of the first bombs had landed nearby and the house had collapsed with the family inside. Private

Davis, serving with the army, had escaped the bombing but returned home on compassionate leave. He spent the week at the site, looking for his family. On the Friday evening some small, unidentifiable remains had been found. However, there had been other people in the house and the remains could not be definitely identified as being from Private Davis' family. Then on Saturday morning he found the bodies of his wife and two daughters, aged five and two. His wife could only be identified by her wedding ring. Next day he found his son John, aged five weeks. On the top storey of a house hit early in the raid, the family could have had no time to take cover. Death must have been instantaneous. Another soldier who came home to find his family wiped out was Mr. Ford, whose family had lived in New King Street. Anne Marks, who lived nearby, remembers seeing him:

> I remember their father coming home on compassionate leave and seeing him kneeling, crying at the remains on the pavement when they dug the bodies out a week later. They were covered with a tarpaulin, but you could see the small, rigid huddles underneath.

Albert Davis was also at work in the Kingsmead area:

> At New King Street there was a house clean knocked out. Still up there was a fireplace and a clock still ticking. You could go into a house half-blitzed and still see cups and saucers completely unmoved. We had a call to go to Green Park. The walls were standing but there was no inside. Noises were heard in the basement. It was a heap of rubble but we had to communicate. If there were any pipes that came up through, we could first call for silence and cordon off the roads. Then we would tap the pipe and they would tap back. A mate of mine lived there. I told my chaps to go carefully. I was tapping and the lads were listening in a circle. I heard tapping and looked up but it was my mate: the tapping had been kids tapping behind the house.

At Kingsmead Terrace there were people trapped in the cellar. We could hear tapping. We got a bloke out safe from under the stairs but he died coming downstairs. We put him on a stretcher. An old lady came up with chocolate for him. I knocked her aside. It was dangerous and he might have abdominal injuries. The old woman swore at me – she thought I was cruel ... At one incident one old lady's house was hit. She usually hid behind the piano and was buried there. We found her there, without a stitch. But she wouldn't come out without her shoes. She didn't mind the rest. I had to rummage around for a pair of shoes and lend her my overcoat.

It was always stupid to open the door straightaway: you didn't know what was above. This happened to me at an incident at Margaret's Buildings where the end was blown down. We knew there were two men trapped in the cellar as we were told they had been seen running towards there. It was one heap of rubble. I was the party leader and looked next door, a hairdresser's, which was still standing. I had a lifeline around me, a sash-cord held by another man so I could pull it if in danger. I went up to the door of the barber's shop so as to go down through the cellar wall. The door was half open. I opened it gently, frightened, and something fell on me. It was a dressmaker's dummy. We got the men out, but they were dead.

Opposite was Catherine Place which was made up of big houses. We were told there were eight people trapped there. The end house was down, but not straight – the top floors were overhanging. I sent men in. The leader shouldn't be involved and I watched in case the walls fell. I was doing this when one of my chaps came up and said his employer was the owner of the house, and he wanted to see me. The owner said that if my man could get a tank down from the floor above ... I told him I'd put a hatchet through his head. He reported me. Next day we were looking for one man there and the owner said my men were working in perilous conditions. I told him what I thought of him. Eventually, a man came up and said it was he – he'd been to hospital, been discharged and hadn't thought of notifying the police that he was alright.

At the top of Stanley Road there was a shop. There was an air raid shelter in the road there. Two women from the shop were missing. We went through the rubble and only found a piece of one's frock. We looked across: in the house, the windows were out. We looked in and there was a hole in the boards. We thought we could see a bomb sticking out. The bomb disposal bloke came. He went over the windowsill and put his stethoscope to it. He found it was a piece of iron with rings around it.

The biggest and longest incident was the half destroyed Regina Hotel. Mr. Hamlin felt that the rescue services should never have needed to go there in the first place. If everyone had gone to the basement shelter then they might have survived. Those in the basement had simply walked out, unharmed, the following morning. Soldiers assisted the rescue squads as they worked methodically through the rubble that comprised the demolished half of the hotel. Bodies were brought out every day. Once again, a soldier returned home to find his family destroyed. Lieutenant Murray of the Gordon Highlanders had his parents brought from the wreckage of the Regina on the Monday. His wife was found still alive. She died in hospital three days later. Lady Shand's body was found on the 29th; the Reverend Woodmansey's was finally uncovered on the 1st May. Mr. Davis was also working at this site:

At the Regina, Colonel Johnson and his wife were killed. His daughter lived nearby. If we found jewellery, we could hand it over if the person gave sufficient identification. I found a jewellery box there with Mrs. Johnson's name. A woman in nurse's uniform came down, the daughter's companion, asking if the Colonel was found. A few days later, they brought out the jewellery case and I sent for the nurse. I showed the case to her and on my instructions she went back and got authority from the daughter. I sent a despatch rider to get the policeman as witness. I took the nurse to the part of the hotel still standing and asked her to describe each piece of jewellery so the policeman and I could write it down and check it. We then signed each other's book as a safety check.

If we couldn't prove an identity, we put the valuables in a debris basket and at the end of the day would hand over each piece to the depot supervisor who checked them and put them into a deed box. Both of us would sign each other's book and the goods were sent to the Lost Property Office at the Guildhall. I found the will of Colonel Howard and sent it down to the Guildhall. I was pestered by a firm of solicitors as to whether I had found it. After about three weeks, I got fed up with my time being wasted. A week later they found the will. They had taken the deed boxes beforehand, shaken them and not heard the paper. The Colonel's daughter had been in India and then came to Bath. She left after the blitz and went to Bournemouth.

At the Regina, a chap came up and I asked who he was. He said his friend was a butler there. I said he was alright. He'd brought up beer for him, but the latter had gone. I said to the policeman that he had offered the drink to the men, so that he couldn't say we had taken it. The policeman sampled it first. I kept my eyes open. I saw one bloke again. I went to the policeman about him. The policeman challenged him, and he said he was an Hon. He said he was the guardian of the two Misses Corfield. I said they were both dead, but he proved that one was alive. The other sister was buried there. I asked if he could get the sister to identify the body. He and the woman came up. In a room was the body under a blanket. I pulled it up and she identified the body. The woman asked me, as in shock, to give her the pearls off the neck. But I said she would have to do it. She said she couldn't do it, nor could the guardian. So I told the undertaker to remove them. Two days after this, the Hon. came up with a brown paper parcel to see me. He'd thought things over and had brought up some cigarettes for the men. I called a policeman to witness this. I was only doing my duty, I said.

You had to be very careful when people were under shock. People would offer you money and not know they were doing it. You could easily fall into traps. There was always someone out to trap you ... You had to stop, think, act. I suppose I took about a dozen debris bags of jewellery from the Regina. It was up to the people to claim stuff from the Guildhall then. Even then, you had to be careful. Occasionally you deliberately showed someone a different brooch, for instance, to prove if someone was on the fiddle ... I saw a bloke at the hotel with six handbags. I stopped him. The bloke went hysterical. I slapped his face. He said they were his family's handbags and the names were all the same, and that that was his name. But we had to be sure. He cooled down anyway. A rescue party came in from one place outside Bath with a proper rescue van and looted. I had five bodies laid out at the Regina one night. I was worn out and asked a policeman to watch them while we rested.

A number of bodies were unidentified when brought from the hotel. At least 27 people died there, though. The problem of dealing with distraught relatives and valuable possessions was one faced by a number of the rescue services. The Home Guard were on patrol in the worst bombed areas with rifles and live ammunition. Leslie Nott crossed swords with one official over the question of valuables:

Two days after the raids I went to Elm Grove Terrace where we got four bodies out. One old gentleman had £800 on him. This was given to me to take to some special place, I forget its name, at the Guildhall. I handed it in and said it had been found by Harry Head. The woman there said that was alright but also said that we had to bring anything valuable in. I think she wanted some work.

Next I went to Cheltenham Street. Something shiny

came up. It was the head and the handle of an axe. The owner had been a woodcutter who had been presented with this silver-topped, engraved axe when he retired. So I said it was valuable. It was very enjoyable to carry it into the Guildhall and plonk it down in front of this woman. She asked me why I had brought it. I said you asked for anything valuable to be brought in.

Bodies were still being brought in as well. A number of ambulance men were sent along to clear out the Scala shelter. The bodies were taken to the mortuary where they were stripped, stacked and then hosed down. Some could not be carried off in this way. Pieces of bodies were raked out and picked up from the soil around the shelter. Some were put in biscuit tins, others into sheets and taken to the mortuary; but it was hopeless to try to identify them and they were taken straight out to the communal grave. A number of bodies were identified by possessions rather than by seeing the actual person. One man recognised his brother, killed at the Scala shelter, by being shown his police pocket book. Some bodies were identified this way, not because they were otherwise unidentifiable, but in order to spare the relatives further shock and sadness. Positive identification would then lead to a label being put on to the body and an inventory taken of their clothing and effects. The WVS patched up some bodies so that relatives could identify them. When no one came forward, this inventory might still prove useful at some later date. A head and shoulders photograph might also be taken to aid future identification. One small two-year old girl who died in hospital was described in the newspaper as having greyish blue eyes and fair hair. A full description was given, but she was still buried unidentified. Another dozen or so were buried unidentified. A slightly larger number were labelled unidentifiable. These were the bodies that were too greatly mutilated to be identified. Some, like those picked up from the Scala shelter, were only pieces of bodies. The blast was so great, in such a confined space, that at least seven bodies were unidentifiable. One could not be recognised as anything human. All that was left was a cigarette case, a photo and one pair of gloves. Another yielded only a portion of clothing, thought to belong to a young woman. The bomb that landed in St. James' cemetery had scattered a number of grave stones. Jill Clayton's father had to help clear up the mess, including a number of disturbed skeletons. At least one portion of scalp was discovered that may have come from a missing woman or simply have been blown from an old grave.

The casualties continued to mount up long after the raids had finished. One old woman, found wandering in Victoria Park, was taken to hospital but died there soon after. John O'Shea died in hospital after being dug out from Roseberry Road. Sydney Poole's parents, rescued from the shelter in Stanley Road, both died within a week of the raids. The bodies piled up at some mortuaries: Weymouth House dealt with 174 in all. Doris Smith, another ambulance driver, took bodies from the RUH:

> I took corpses to Weymouth House School. Legs, arms, etc. were brought out. I had two 'loaned' Colerne young airforce boys and their lorry. We brought one lot out in a great laundry basket. The two boys went yellow. Two part timers had to get some stiffs, but they said they only had two stretchers. I told them to pile them up. They were shocked, but we couldn't go by respect then.

The large number of dead put a great strain on the appropriate authorities. The London investigators felt that after the first 24 hours, Bath had coped well. Even so, the long set of forms could not always be completed in full. Some death certificates were duplicated. Luckily there were few cases such as the one the warden Shearn encountered on the first night of the raids. Then he had been looking along a row of dead bodies when he noticed a movement amongst them. One girl had only been knocked out and was definitely not dead. William Smith, as an ambulance driver, had many experiences of dealing with corpses:

> There was no question of inquests: it was 'death due
> to enemy action'. The bodies were certified dead at the
> mortuaries – normally 'not on' even in wartime – and not
> just at the hospitals. After all, if a body was picked up without
> its head, it couldn't be alive. They had dead labels put on
> them, giving details of where they were found. They were
> moved to Weymouth House School and kept there awaiting
> identification, and eventual burial. As far as possible, bodies
> were listed as to where they were found, and then taken
> to the nearest mortuary, for example Oldfield Park bodies
> were taken to St. Peter's. They could be partly identified
> by the site where they were found, although in some cases,
> for example the Regina Hotel, they were visitors to Bath.
> Eventually, a registry was set up in the Guildhall. Bodies
> could be identified through an address by the person who
> picked them up. But in some places, as at the Scala, in
> some cases no one knew who was in a shelter and at the
> Scala they were unidentifiable and ripped to pulp. They
> were brought in in baskets.

On the Wednesday after the raids a call had gone out
for volunteers to man an information bureau in the Abbey
Churchyard. Nine others were set up. The central police
station also took enquiries for missing persons. The Citizens'
Advice Bureau, aided by a number of students from Bristol
University, helped to answer questions about missing persons.
Many enquiries, quite naturally, came from men serving in
the armed forces, worried for the lives of their families who
were in Bath. At the Pump Room a special centre was run by
four army officers to deal solely with military enquiries. 800
telegrams were sent, 200 men were given special leave. Even
so, although people like Mr. Gough and Mr. Ford were given
leave, other soldiers could not get back to Bath. One soldier
who was told that his home town had been bombed was not
sure whether he should thank his informant for this sketchy

information. Certainly he could not check it further, as he was a prisoner of war, held by the Japanese. One dead woman was identified by her brother-in-law, as her husband was serving overseas.

Civilian relatives also had fears that their families had been killed. One man set off from Wales to hunt out members of his family:

> I lived in Cardiff at the time and came to visit relatives in Bath. It was devastated. Kingsmead was completely flattened. The Cardiff train stopped at Bristol and I had to catch a bus to Bath. People in the bus kept on saying 'Oh! I know someone who lived there' and wanting to stop the bus.

Some had to make a number of visits. On Monday, the recently widowed Mrs. Cooper had been picked up from Bath by her sister and niece from Staines. On Wednesday, the niece Joan Taylor and a male colleague went back to Bath to try again to find the body of Mr. Cooper. The body had initially been taken to St. James' Church, but in the confusion when the church caught fire, the fact had not been publicised that all the bodies had been taken to the school next door. Now, two days later, there was less confusion and when Miss Taylor's friend went to the Guildhall he discovered where the bodies had been taken. When he got to the Weymouth House School he discovered a further complication. The bodies had been immersed in water when St. James' caught fire. As a result the identification sheets and labels were completely illegible. Miss Taylor's friend offered to have a look at the bodies instead. The third he looked at was Mr. Cooper and he was allowed to take the body away for private burial.

Mrs. Horler, in Tenby, had to wait until Thursday before she finally received a letter from her mother:

> I received a letter to my relief saying she was alright, the house not damaged, but no water, gas or electric. So I sent

a telegram saying 'Coming to fetch you to stay with us'. I travelled to Bath on the first train, arriving at Bristol. I went to the usual platform for Bath. A porter said: 'No trains to Bath, the line was bombed. Buses outside!'. To get a good view I sat in the front seat of the double decker bus. As we reached Bath the desolation was terrible; rows of houses razed to the ground, huge craters everywhere. I have a vivid memory of an old man sitting in front of his bombed house in an armchair, in tears. Reaching the Abbey, I joined a queue for the Fairfield Park bus. I waited over three-quarters of an hour, in vain. Wishing I had walked, I asked an inspector why the delay, and his reply was: 'It's the funeral today of the victims, a mass funeral. The buses cannot pass all the hearses.'

Alighting by Claremont Methodist Church I could see my friend's pink curtains blowing straight out of the windows, no glass! Believe me, by then I was trembling like a leaf and, when I greeted my mother, found I had completely lost my voice! ... Next morning we set off early to catch the first train to Wales; drank some milk (cold – there was no gas to make tea). Walking along Camden Road the road glistened with 'diamonds' – glass from all the broken windows. Reaching the Lansdown Road, buses were coming down from Lansdown with people who were sleeping on the race course for safety. They were laden with pillows, eiderdowns, cases, food, etc. Never have I enjoyed a cup of tea more than the one we drank at the restaurant of Bristol Temple Meads, and how pleased to reach Tenby ...

The mass funeral that Mrs. Horler mentioned was the largest, but by no means the only burial of the dead. Some were buried privately. Dr. Middlemas was cremated at Bristol, on the Friday. On the Saturday morning the Cutting family of Kingsmead Terrace were buried at Haycombe cemetery. The mass funeral took place later that day at the same cemetery. The Welsh Guards had worked for days to prepare a mass grave. Some coffins were being put down into the long row in the grave as the 25 minute service began. Army lorries had brought the dead from the mortuaries. A fleet of buses ferried the mourners from the Parade Gardens. Immediate friends and relatives were shepherded into a special enclosure, overlooking the plain wooden coffins. Each bore a name, or names, and a number in black paint. A few had no name at all: they were unidentified or unidentifiable. The simply curious were prevented from getting too far into the cemetery and kept away from the service. Two other, smaller, mass burials were conducted in the following week at the same cemetery until there were almost 250 bodies buried there.

On May 2nd, the day after the first mass burial, the city received its first real morale raiser. Taking most people by surprise, the King and Queen paid a visit to Bath. They were received by the Mayor, Alderman Aubrey Bateman and the Regional Commander from Bristol, Sir Hugh Ellis. They then went on a short tour of some of the worst hit areas. They looked around the gutted ruins of the Assembly Rooms. Nearby at the Regina Hotel, the body of Major Oliver was just being brought out and was put in an ambulance as the royal party walked by. In Oldfield Park, the royal couple watched a row of terraces being demolished. They stopped at the Scala shelter. Sam Hayward, the warden, saw them there. They also talked to a number of special constables and to a Mr. Hartley whose father had been killed when taking cover in the shelter. A car took them up to Beechen Cliff where the mayor pointed out some features from this vantage point. Small crowds were gathering by this time, but many were still unaware of the distinguished guests in their midst. Walter Sweetenham was at school on the top of Beechen Cliff when he was later told that the King and Queen had been up and down the avenues there. One woman was surprised when her sons returned home and casually remarked that they had been talking to the Queen on Beechen Cliff. By the time the tour ended, word had got around and large crowds gathered at the Guildhall. Here the royal couple talked to some of the councillors and the Civil Defence leaders. Dr. Astley-Weston was asked by the King as to how the soft and dusty Bath stone had stood up to the bombing.

In a packed 1½ hours the couple had been both north and south of the river, met the people and talked to the local leaders. The Queen left three huge parcels of tea, blankets and clothes and then it was time for them to go.

CHAPTER ELEVEN

Clearing Up

The raids on Exeter had been the first large-scale German bombing effort of 1942. As a result, they drew much comment in the British newspapers. However, damage, so far, had been slight and Bath attracted far more attention, owing to the scale of the destruction there. Not all the national newspapers were particularly sympathetic, however. At least one London paper commented on the supposed lack of Civil Defence preparations in Bath: an accusation that the mayor vigorously denied. A more general view, hinted at by most of the London press, was that this raid was proof that nowhere was safe from attack. So far, so good, but there was also the suggestion in some papers that the war had finally reached those who had tried to escape it: rich evacuees who had fled to Bath had finally been caught up in the war. The city had believed it was free from attack: now it would be a lesson to so many other towns that had felt little concern about the war. The implication that Bath had done little to help in the war effort was obvious.

In fact, this was not a new comment. Before 1942, accusation and counter-accusation had flown about whether Bath had contributed enough to various war funds. In 1944 the city was accused of refusing to take in a new wave of refugees fleeing from the V1 flying bomb attacks in London. Yet by and large the city did fulfill its duties and did make a valid contribution. Some people had come down from London for the duration of the war. Yet the bombs had landed on the working class areas of Twerton and Oldfield Park, and on the rich hotels in the centre of the city. In the final death toll, a mere handful were listed as having come from obvious target cities such as London. Bath was a major West Country town with, or without, evacuees. Just because a city had not been regularly bombed did not mean it had felt it could ignore the war.

One other aspect rubbed salt into Bath's wounds. As a famous city and the first devastated target of 1942, Bath drew a great deal of attention, and not just in the press. Ministries and newspapers repeatedly asked people not to travel to Bath unless it was absolutely necessary. Transport was still in some disarray and 'phone communications were liable to disruption. If there were worries about relatives there, then one could look at casualty lists published in Bristol, for example. Some people, unable to contact relatives and not seeing them on the casualty lists, would have to travel to Bath. However, there were also large numbers of people who just came to sightsee. Leslie Nott remembers them as being a real nuisance. A London investigator described them as becoming 'exceptionally menacing'. The flood of intruders became so great that one WVS administrator felt it necessary to write a letter to the *Times*. Those who had suffered, she wrote, deeply resented the presence of sightseers. Bombed-out people could cope with most things except for the fact that others were walking around just looking at the damage.

For even with the casualties rescued and most bodies accounted for, there was still plenty of work to be done. If people could be dragged from the ruins of their houses, then it was possible that some household effects might also be rescued from the debris of stone, wood and plaster. Much would undoubtedly be destroyed, however, and the surviving items buried far beneath the rubble. Kathleen Muse's father returned to the remains of their house in Beechen Cliff Place and managed to rescue two teddy bears. Hubert Jackson had more luck picking around the ruins of his house, although he found it was sometimes the strangest and most fragile objects that survived:

I came down to see if I could retrieve anything. My wife said: 'Well I never did like the furniture.' The lampstand was the only thing we saved. I had a scarf on a hook on a door. When we got out of the shelter, the scarf wasn't there. It was neatly under the bottom bar of the shelter, half underneath. The shelter must have gone right up so that the scarf and the rubble went under it. I used to belong to the Admiralty Home Guard. They arrived to help and said they'd saved my eggs (for preserving). We had had them in the bathroom and the whole lot must have gone down neatly. Not one was broken. A Woolworth lamp in the kitchen that I recovered was still alright. When the house was being rebuilt one of the workmen found my box camera, with a film inside. It was given to my neighbour who then gave it to me. The film was still in there and I had it developed; it still developed alright. I had a radio on the writing set in the corner. It was thrown into the debris and when I examined it later, all I had to do was to get some sticky tape and join up the speaker to the frame and it was okay.

My sister-in-law, whose husband was a naval officer, asked us to mind her husband's medals. We had them in a case, in the front boxroom. We'd forgotten about it. When we told her we had lost the house, she asked if we had retrieved the medals. But that part of the house was gone. Months later I happened to walk up the garden and looked back towards the house. The sun was shining and caused a sort of glitter. Somebody came around – people were very helpful – and got on top of the rubble and found it was a case. He also found a lot of soap up there, between and among the beams. When the house was blown up, we had a wardrobe in the corner upstairs. It must have just slid into the same position downstairs. We used to come down to see what we could retrieve. We found a wardrobe with a smashed door. Despite the fact that the doors were closed, I was getting my suits out and finding they were perfect. But when I put my hands in the pockets there was glass in them – very little pieces.

One woman returned from Bristol to her home to find it partially demolished. Soldiers had rescued a few belongings and piled them up in the street. A woman opposite had rescued a sewing machine and put it in her house for safety. This was a useful safeguard. Looting was never an epidemic, but it occurred in sufficient cases for it to be worthwhile to take care of one's possessions. In many ways it depended on what one meant by the term, 'looting'. A house opposite the Homestead First Aid Post was bombed and at least one man died there. Grace Selwyn was temporarily shocked when an American nurse walked into the ruined house and plucked a number of roses from the garden. The idea that one could take much needed equipment from obviously abandoned houses was one that took hold in some quarters. It was an idea that did seem to make sense. Robert Smith was involved in taking items from the same house that the nurse had walked into:

We had moved to the Homestead. The house opposite was blitzed; a lady warden said we could use anything in it to furnish our damaged housing quarters. Beds and bedding, and so on were removed. I made a report of this for the Guildhall and thought that was alright. However, it was reported to the police and eventually we had to go before the Chief Constable. I said a letter had been typed, but it hadn't been typed and the girl letter writer was sent for. She removed the letter from a locked cabinet and this cleared us. Eventually the stuff was taken to Frome. The owner of the house was in South Africa and apparently the warden didn't have the right to take the stuff.

Kathleen Muse and her family had taken clothes from shattered windows in the centre of town, but it did seem an urgent necessity at the time. Anne Marks and her friends scoured the Kingsmead area, as children did in many parts of the city:

Later on, in the summer when things settled down, the 'looting' started. We kids – remember New King Street was a rough area – went on long hunts through the ravaged ruins. We were starved of toys, because of the war. Our best haul was from under New King Street Methodist Church, on the site of Percy Boys' Club, where we found several double-jointed dolls ... children's books, beach balls and clockwork toys. Maybe we shouldn't have taken them, but it was very damp and we told ourselves that they would only spoil if we left them there. We told our mothers that we bought them at a jumble sale. I was also on hand when the demolition agents moved in to knock down Number 8, New King Street which had only been partly demolished by the direct hit on Number 7. I knew that the girls who had lived on the top floor had owned a lot of toys, and I dashed in, as the house fell, to retrieve a load of comics that came fluttering down. You should have heard what the workmen called me.

Such searching was not only dangerous, but sometimes rather harrowing as well. Looking through the rubble on the site of Kingsmead School, Mrs. Marks unearthed a shoe that she recognised as having belonged to a friend killed in the bombing. Only ruins and partially demolished houses were searched, however. Damaged houses that were obviously still inhabited were usually left alone. Marjorie Horsell did not leave the Homestead until the Wednesday after the raids. She found her home had lost all its windows and doors but nothing had been taken. Even on shattered sites, the law said that nothing should be taken by any individual; even at major sites such as the Regina Hotel, the rescue workers had to be very careful to itemise every piece of equipment that was found. The Home Guard carried loaded rifles. The police had pistols, although ammunition was not issued for them. The laws concerning looting were severe. They could carry the death penalty. This was never applied, though, and most cases were minor. The local paper carried the occasional story of people being tried for looting. On May 16th, a 60 year old man was sentenced to four months hard labour for picking up around £6 of coins from one site. In his defence, the man claimed he had only been looking for souvenirs. A more nimble-fingered thief was encountered by Henry Gough:

My wife's house was blown to the ground. It's hard to imagine it as everything had gone. The slates flew. There were huge blocks of Bath stone which had fallen in. I tried to clear them. There was a pile of rubble. I lifted two or three stones but there was a whole storey's worth. I knew where the wife's presents were – we were saving up. I found one glass from a Stewart glass set. I salvaged the sewing machine which had been in the room above the shelter. I also found the typewriter. My wife said that a double mattress had been brought and put in the shelter. I worked hard to get it. My fingers were bleeding but I got to the mattress and got it out by moving the stone ... I pulled it towards the side of the road and left it on the edge of a rough pathway. I went to the hole to get some clothes and when I came back it was gone. The odd person did this sort of thing.

Next door, Mr. Russell was a paper seller. He saved coins and never banked them. He kept farthings everywhere in sugar packets, filled with coins. He had piles of pound notes that were all destroyed. The coins were tossed up in the air. There was a court case about them being picked up.

It is difficult to say how far such looting was organised. Official records make mention of supposed rescue squads that came from outside, but took no part in any rescue work. They spent a few days in the city and then left. Eric Davies became involved in a case of looting that spread further than the city of Bath:

I lost everything in the blitz ... we lost every stick of furniture, bar one chair. No one could find anything – not even my gun. I had to verify it was gone with the local police at Twerton, so that I could get new army kit.

My brother got a bath out from our home. He salvaged some other goods from the house, put them in the bath and covered them with a rug. But a dress and other things and ornaments were taken from there. The people who took them were from London. My uncle was in a pub and heard them arranging for transport and when the lorry would pick the stuff up. They'd taken our stuff, and others, to Clyde Buildings. My uncle heard there was stuff in that house already and it was going to London. I contacted the CID and they sent two men down. We went to the house and a detective forced the lock. In the house I recognised a clock which was the landlord's. He wasn't interested, but I was incensed. What we'd dug out in the bath was gone ...

But the men claimed they'd dug me out. I had no witnesses. The people swore they helped to dig us out. I didn't want to take action if they had helped rescue me. I later found they hadn't, but I was on the spot. Then, I didn't know who dug us out. We found the dress. One of their wives was wearing the dress in an East End pub. It was a big bit in the paper at the time. I seemed the villain of the piece. My wife got her dress back and a couple of saucepans and other things.

A local paper carried the story of the trial under the heading: 'Blitz heroine on loot charge'. It reported that the woman had been given the bath by workers at the site as she wanted it for her children. The dress had been thrown to her. This and the other items in the bath were taken to a house in Clyde Buildings. She claimed her husband knew nothing of this. She also presented other peoples' testimonies as to her bravery in helping to rescue people. Suitably impressed, the bench had said there were 'special circumstances' in this case and she was merely bound over to appear for judgment, if recalled, in the next 12 months. Some of the goods were returned. The woman was not recalled and had no further punishment.

Mr. Davies eventually received £12 from the Mayor's fund towards the cost of replacing some of his lost property. A woman had walked into the office of the *Evening Chronicle* on the first Monday after the raids to hand in a few pennies for those who had suffered. Money was soon coming in from a large number of sources. The town of Bath, in America, and the Emperor Haile Selassie of Ethiopia, who had lived temporarily in Bath after Mussolini invaded his homeland, sent messages and donations. By May 25th the fund already stood at £24,000. More was to come in. The government itself would pay the bulk of money for damages. Even so, the amount of work one had to do to replace lost documents and items was enough to daunt anyone, let alone someone still recovering from the destruction of their home. Mobile laundries were set up. Free clothes could be picked up from the rest centres. Furniture that could be salvaged was to be labelled and left outside. The council would pick it up and store it until new accommodation was available. Claims for damage to clothes, furniture and houses all needed the appropriate forms. If one had lost important documents, then there were busy days ahead. Replacement national insurance cards were available from the Post Office. Identity cards could be had from the Guildhall. Ration books could be got from the Octagon in Milsom Street. Financial aid was available from the employment exchange, but here the situation was complicated by the fact that after damage by fire, it had had to move from Kingsmead to new premises on the Upper Bristol Road. In cases of extreme want, where people had lost everything, a mobile assistance board was set up to issue immediate grants of up to £10. In particular, wives of soldiers whose husbands were abroad were often in difficulty and needed help.

First aid repairs to houses were done as soon as possible by council and other workmen. Edwin Stainer's parents' house had frosted glass put in to replace their smashed windows. Bernard Humphries' father, the cabinet worker, was unable to find any of his tools in the wreckage of the works and was co-opted into helping with building work. Temporary window boards and a tarpaulin on the roof were later replaced by more permanent work. More forms had to be sent to the appropriate authorities to claim money for the work done. At the City of Bath Boys' School there was some disruption of lessons as a number of the internal walls had collapsed and needed rebuilding. Walter Sweetenham and his class had to troop down to the less damaged girls' school for some lessons. By the middle of June there were still 2,500 men working on repairs to buildings in Bath. The scenes of greatest devastation were merely tidied up: the debris was piled up on to the site and left to a later time. Anne Marks remembers seeing large bushes of the shrub buddleia growing throughout the Kingsmead area. Damaged buildings were brought down if considered a danger. The cupola and clock of St. James' Church were pulled down by soldiers. In June the bomb-damaged tower of Apsley House was knocked down as well.

Some people, their houses destroyed, had to find new places in which to live. Hubert Jackson stayed with friends in Mount Road for a week or so. Then the WVS helped them to find more permanent accommodation. A woman in Southdown had a top flat empty and they lived there until the end of the war. Kathleen Muse and her family were also aided:

There were too many people, first at Swainswick and then Marshfield. We stayed with different relatives to get away from town. We then had to sign in to the council to find accommodation and were billeted up at Odd Down. We were just given an address to go to. People were given addresses of free houses. It was in Odins Road and owned by one of mother's friends who was just off to the country. She was kindness itself.

Other families were able to take over houses of friends and relatives who had decided to leave the city. Muriel Gough's family lived in a friend's home when the friend went to stay in a country cottage for a while. Florence Delve, staying with her mother in Wales, received a letter from her husband:

My husband had to come back to Bath to work. One day, he and a neighbour were going along Sion Hill when they went past a house there and discovered it was empty. They decided to dig out what furniture they could and then squatted there. My husband wrote me this. Six weeks after the raids I came back and we all squatted there.

THE BOMBING OF BATH

The danger had not ended with the all-clear after the second raid. At least 36 bombs had failed to explode, 5% of those that had fallen. It was later said that the bombers had dropped many bombs so low that they had not exploded. The one at St. James's Parade had been removed quickly. One that fell near the Old Bridge had still managed to cause damage by slicing through the electricity cable there. None exploded while being removed, but some did cause difficulty. A series of bombs fell in parkland at the top above Victoria Park and proceeded to settle further down into the soft earth. The bomb disposal men took until 1944 before they concluded that all bombs were out from there and that claims of more bombs on the site could be discredited. Some turned out to be false alarms. Others could not be verified, such as the bomb that was said to have fallen into the river beside Pulteney Bridge. The unexploded bombs could cause discomfort. One that landed caused all the houses in Lyncombe Vale to be evacuated. A Mrs. Wicks decided to stay put and her family slept on deck chairs in the basement for a week. A group of evacuees in the same house slept in the basement kitchen, dressed in their outdoor gear and with the ladies clutching at their handbags.

Other people were still affected by the attacks. Many spent some time in hospital. Doreen Wall was in hospital for a number of months:

I was in there for about 12 weeks. The sirens went a lot. I had to have three operations on my knee as it was smashed up inside and it had to be opened up. I went to the operating theatre three Saturdays in a row: my leg was in half-plaster. I was examined by a bone specialist who said that as I was so young, it had to be done right. It did eventually get better and I could even ride a bike. I saw a lot of things in there I wouldn't have expected to have seen in those days. Many people died. My father was in the men's ward. When I was well enough I visited him in a chair so that we could talk. He was in much longer than me, with a thigh injury ... As soon as they could see I could walk, I only stayed another week. I had to go back once a month.

The most unpopular task that still required the services of the Civil Defence units was the continuing search for bodies. In most cases, it was not a matter of continually combing through the rubble, but of answering a specific request, as William Smith found:

We were still removing bodies up to three months afterwards, which was not a very pleasant job. After a while, the sites were tidied up, but we would get complaints of a nasty smell in the area. We would find the body by the smell. We would go to the incident, perhaps sit there for half an hour on a stone and watch for flies. We were issued with rum for that job and I can't bear the smell now.

Vic Penny was involved in a similar case:

I was in Julian Road, in July I think, with an old chap in the ambulance service, Walter Watts ... we had a call from Bath Corporation. They were clearing rubble in Julian Road in front of the Catholic Church. They'd found what they thought could be a body. It was a very hot day and it had been there for four months. A long way from it you could smell it. The council workmen had left it – you could just see a hand and clothes. We had to pick it up by the clothes as it was too decomposed to touch. It took one or two hours. No one helped! The landlord of the Chequers in Rivers Street brought along a tray with a bottle of whisky and two glasses. It was a very unpleasant thing to do. The smell was absolutely atrocious. We almost went back to get the gasmasks. We did have to get our handkerchiefs. The body was taken to the city mortuary, under the arches at the old bridge.

In a few cases a particular body was being hunted. But even if it was found, positive identification was not always possible after a number of weeks, as Leslie Nott found out:

> We were looking for someone down Cheltenham Street for some three weeks after the raids. We found a man and woman, sat upright in their chairs, arm-in-arm, just skeletons. They had been eaten to pieces by rats.

At the same time other scraps were found in the same area. Small pieces of remains were found at one house and a portion of a brown coat at 36 Cheltenham Street. Books discovered at the same site suggested at least one person had come from Comfortable Place. The last remains were, in fact, removed from Cheltenham Street on the 19th May. The rescue parties had been withdrawn a week earlier.

The raids permanently changed the habits of some people. No one ignored the sirens in future. Many slept fully dressed and took whistles down to their shelters, to signal for aid if the house was demolished. On damaged houses that were still inhabited, a chalk mark would be put outside. This indicated the number of people who were living there. Some numbers were changed by young children though. Trekking continued for months. This was hardly surprising, as both Exeter and Norwich suffered return attacks during this series of raids. Doris Smith, who had sheltered in the railway tunnel, spent three weeks on a friend's farm. The Whiteleys' home at Hanover Street had been damaged and the family stayed out of the city in a farm until July. However, the Germans did not return and there was never another death by bombing in Bath.

The German raids on the cathedral cities continued for another month or so. Norwich was attacked after Bath. York lost its ancient Guildhall. Canterbury and Exeter lost large areas of medieval buildings. No city suffered as many casualties as Bath. Then the attacks petered out. The Luftwaffe returned to the 'tip and run' raids whereby a handful of aircraft would machine-gun and bomb a coastal resort and fly off as soon as possible. It was all they could manage. While the main raids were still on, some British newspapers had feared that Bomber Command might stop bombing industrial Germany in order to save cities such as Bath. But the RAF never overestimated the German threat. Many of the German aircraft had come from the training units. The Luftwaffe could not afford to lose its instructors. Even if they survived the raids, then much valuable instruction time had been lost. Quite simply, the Germans could not afford to maintain these raids for any great length of time.

In terms of confusion caused and publicity gained, the raids had been a minor success. More newspaper coverage was given to an unexpected raid on historic Bath than might have been given, say, to yet another attack on the vast metropolis of London. Proportionally more damage could be done to a smaller target like Bath, and the Germans could still try to claim they were capable of delivering knock out blows in the west. But Baron von Sturm's unfortunate allusion to three star cities in the Baedeker guidebooks meant that Germany had lost the propaganda war, at least as far as world opinion was concerned. In Germany, a recent biography of Goebbels inverts the truth by saying that the Baedeker raids were a series of attacks on German cultural centres such as Lübeck. But Goebbels himself realised who had made the mistake and severely criticised the Foreign Office for the slip. He admitted, privately, that British cultural centres were being attacked but disliked the way that certain people were glorifying this action.

It made no difference. As far as most people were concerned, Lübeck, when remembered, had been a legitimate target; Bath, and the other cathedral cities, were just old, non-military targets. Few questioned this view. On the Wednesday after the raids, the MP Mr. Rhys Davies asked in parliament whether the attack on Lübeck had been directed against military targets. The destruction, he said, had been terrible. All that provoked in the House were cries of 'What about Bath?' Throughout May and June, British bombers dropped leaflets on German cities. They reproduced a German report on the destruction in Lübeck, as a warning of what was to come. They also bore a copy of Hitler's promise, made early in the war, that any British attack would be met by an overwhelming German response. Both sides knew this was impossible. In early May, Churchill made a most illuminating speech. The raids would continue on Germany. Other munition cities would suffer as Lübeck had done. The German workers could flee to the hills and watch their cities burn; it was the nearest that the government came to admitting that German houses might be bombed, and civilians killed, as well as factories destroyed.

The Baedeker raids were no more than a weak German response to the first stage in Bomber Command's increasingly effective offensive on Germany. It cannot be said that the bombing of Bath had any real effect on the course of the war. Curiously, it had also failed the Germans' primary objective of destroying cultural targets in Bath. There had been plenty of destruction, but mostly in the western suburbs. The Georgian heart of the city had been left largely untouched. The pre-Georgian Abbey Church House had lost its frontage. Half of the south side of Queen Square, the Francis Hotel, had been demolished. Part of Lansdown Crescent had lost its front as the result of blast. Elsewhere, a few Georgian houses had been gutted. Individual houses in the Circus, the Royal Crescent and Somerset Place had been burnt out. So had the Assembly Rooms and one wing of Green Park.

Yet the general damage was severe. 329 houses and shops were totally destroyed, 732 had to be demolished. In all, some 19,147 buildings suffered some degree of damage. Even if this meant that only the windows were blown in, still a substantial proportion of Bath's buildings had suffered some degree of damage. Over 11,000 houses had been repaired by 1944 and thousands more were still awaiting attention. One list of bombs dropped suggested that 323 high-explosive bombs had fallen in and around the city. The destruction was immense but, even in a city, bombs could fall in open spaces. It was calculated that 31 of the heaviest 1,000 kg bombs had fallen. 15 hit buildings, 3 landed in the roads; but 13 wasted themselves on open ground. The statistics are not always accurate. Bombs could only be estimated by the size of the crater that was left and the neat bomb census compiled after the raids was later criticised in some quarters for inaccuracy. The casualty lists may also be inaccurate. Obviously the deaths accumulated as the days passed: 374 by May 5th, 392 by the 15th. A final figure of 417 was later quoted. This may, however, be the total for all raids during the war, the two raids in 1941 included. The death certificates include at least one name that is duplicated. A year or so later, the local authorities noted from the In Memoriam column in the *Evening Chronicle* a list of ten or so names. They were the dead who did not appear in the Civilian War Deaths registers. They include the two members of the Poole family, mother and daughter-in-law. Two more names were added to those who died at 32 Kingsmead Street. In the confusion after the raids, one body had been removed from a demolished house by the rescue services and put on a bed. It had then been removed from the bed and had not been seen again. It must be assumed that those that were never found equalled the number that were buried unidentified or unidentifiable. Yet the comparison is difficult. It was not until 1946 that the photograph of one dead man was identified. A Patrick Murray had been in the Merchant Navy. His ship was in port and he had gone to Bath for the evening. There he had been killed. His father not having heard from him for three years, finally enquired in Bath and identified his son's photograph. It can be assumed at least 400 people did die as a direct result of the raids.

One story can be discounted. The idea that bodies were left at certain incidents and lime, or some other substance, put over them was one particularly mentioned in relation to the Scala shelter. This story, of shelters blocked up and left, as at Coventry, crops up in many cities and never seems to be based on fact. The ambulance men who were at the Scala shelter are sure every piece of body was removed. The smell of remains made sure that any body under rubble would be discovered, and all piles of rubble have long been cleared. Other stories have circulated that are not wholly correct. Accounts are told of German aircraft crashing, at Newbridge, for example. In fact, no enemy aircraft crashed near Bath during the raids. Some did crash at other times and the bodies of their crews are at Haycombe cemetery, but these were separate events. The local squadrons, 87 and 125, at Colerne and Charmy Down, did make attempts to intercept the raiders. At night and in fights that extended well above and beyond the city, they could hardly be seen by people in the city below. That they did badly was no reflection on their ability; quite simply, the equipment, radar in particular, was not sophisticated enough to maintain contact with the German bombers. Even the best pilots with the latest equipment could do relatively little, at this time. 307 Squadron was one of the most experienced; and perhaps this Exeter based squadron answers another question. Stories were told that Polish fighters had helped destroy bombers attacking Bath, and at least two of the squadron's aircraft landed on airfields near Bath.

It is impossible to say which was the first bomb that landed on Bath, especially as fire bombs were in the opening salvos and they were very light. Of the 400 odd deaths, well over 300 were caused by high-explosive bombs. Another 40 died indirectly from the same reason when they were crushed by falling masonry. Six died by fire; again largely because they were trapped in demolished and burning houses. 18 died from unspecified causes. Only three died from machine-gunning: the three soldiers at Mary Magdalene chapel. A lot of bullets were fired, but to cause panic and keep heads down. They may have seemed to be deliberately aimed; this can have rarely been the case. All known unexploded bombs were removed. Some do occasionally turn up, but in unreachable spots such as local waterways, and most are just the small incendiary devices.

The raid took place as a simple revenge raid for the British attack on Lübeck. There are stories that Lord Haw-Haw, the Nazi sympathiser who broadcast to Britain, stated that the Admiralty had moved to Bath. Other broadcasts claimed that

High British staffs were in the city: but revenge was the only motive mentioned in the German orders. One man was later prosecuted in Bath for repeating a story of Lord Haw-Haw's, that the Germans would return to bomb Milsom Street, the high class shopping area, but nothing ever came of it. One or two other stories have been repeated, without full explanation. A number of bomb victims ascribed their bad luck to there being greenhouses near their homes. The German bombers saw the glass, the story goes, and thought it meant factories and so they dropped their bombs. This may be true. Another bomber story refers to the obvious question of how the Abbey escaped serious damage. Such a large target must have been visible from the air. But all the cathedrals in this series of raids escaped major damage, albeit very closely in some cases. Perhaps the Abbey was deliberately left, as the gutting of Coventry Cathedral had proved a great propaganda blow to the Germans. As we have seen, the German High Command wanted to bomb cultural targets without, at first, being seen to do so. Perhaps that is why the Abbey survived.

Most accounts in these pages have been offered by more than one person and checked, as far as possible, with others. Yet one story, continually encountered, has been omitted. It is one of the most famous. At the Scala, it is said, a week or so after the raid, a flock of birds was seen flying around the roof of the cinema. A ladder was eventually put up and on the roof was found the body of a man, supposedly blown from the Scala shelter. It is an intriguing story. Yet no one involved in cleaning up from the shelter makes any mention of it. Those who know of it never seem to know anyone who was actually there. If one goes to the site, it is hard to imagine how a body could be blown all that way. The roof is clearly visible from the ground; a body up there could hardly go unnoticed. But it is a widespread story and may yet prove to be founded in truth.

Most of the individuals whose narratives feature in this book continued to live in Bath after the raids. Most still do today. A few were more active. Eric Davies returned to his regiment, the Somerset Light Infantry. Like many other soldiers who had been in Bath, or gone there on leave, his return was something of a surprise. It was widely rumoured he was dead. His extended leave, given in Bath, had not got through to his base, and he was almost done for desertion. He spent most of the rest of the war fighting in Italy. James Webster, whose home went up in flames, did not see Bath for a long time. He joined the RAF.

The gutted areas of Bath remained derelict for many years. *A Plan for Bath*, the Abercrombie Report of 1946, envisaged massive rebuilding that would, incidentally, have destroyed much of the south part of the town and even Kingsmead Flats, barely ten years old. The plan was too big. The proposed abattoir in Cheltenham Street was built, however, and other suggestions were adopted piecemeal. The architectural gems were rebuilt as they had been. In many cases, as at the Royal Crescent and the Circus, it just meant in-filling. The Assembly Rooms had been gutted but not flattened. Both they and the Abbey Church House were rebuilt as before. A few old buildings were demolished. The wing of Green Park was lost. St. James' was pulled down, as were a number of other churches and chapels. More destruction was caused by the 1960s mania for urban renewal than by German bombs.

The non-Georgian areas suffered a variety of fates. Kingsmead might anyway have been demolished, as was Southgate in the late 1960s, as an area too run-down to save, although the buildings were early 18th century. The bombing removed any qualms and the area was redeveloped in the late 1950s and early 1960s. Kingsmead Street now runs only a hundred yards before coming to a halt in a car park and a block of flats. The bus station replaced the burnt out area near the railway station at the same time. These were the two main areas of devastation. The Scala shelter reverted to a small patch of green opposite the cinema, now a supermarket. The gap in New King Street was for a long time a car wash, and has now been rebuilt. Roseberry Road is a site for light industry. Elm Grove Terrace, nearby, no longer exists. Nor does Beechen

Cliff Place, redeveloped along with most of Holloway after the war. Woolworth stands on the site of St. James' Church, where the bodies floated in the crypt. The Regina Hotel has been rebuilt and turned into private flats. The Francis, in Queen Square, has also been rebuilt and is still an hotel. It is also one of the very few buildings bearing a plaque to commemorate the raids.

One year after the raids, the City of Bath Girls' School magazine tried to get girls to write of their experiences in the blitz. The replies were few. The magazine mentioned the prevailing atmosphere of boredom and lack of interest in the subject. There is, even now, no public monument to the dead in the raids. After the war, the residents of Queen Square handed over their private garden in the centre of the square to the council, in honour of those who were killed; it would make a good site for some form of memorial. At present, the only real sign is the row of white grave stones at Haycombe cemetery, witness to the 247 bodies laid to rest there in the series of mass burials.

There are mixed feelings from those who survived. A lot of very ordinary people did some extraordinary things. There were acts of great bravery. People did work together and help each other. It was a time when one could feel that one was working for a greater good, in a common cause. Yet, as the bombs fell and each person took cover, there were other emotions as well. Some suffered more than others, but it is worth repeating Florence Delve's words:

The last time I was safe was when I heard that (bomb) whistle. From then on it was a nightmare ...

Comradeship and purpose there was, but the price was very high.

Postscript

The first edition of this book finished with a rather down beat tone in terms of the commemoration of the bombing of Bath. The ensuing twenty years have seen a steady rise in interest in the topic and certainly a greater awareness of the deaths involved; so much so that it was decided that rather than simply tweak the existing book, this whole new final chapter should be added.

A number of straightforward physical changes have occurred. By the early 1980s it was said that almost all the gaps caused by bomb damage had been infilled. This is now most definitely the case. Within the last few years a number of replacement buildings have themselves been renamed or even replaced. Woolworth, built on the site of St. James' Church, has itself become part of history and the store has gone through several changes in ownership. Nearby Southgate has been demolished and replaced by a new shopping centre. Indeed the new centre extends far beyond the original site and takes in the site of the post blitz bus station. The new bus station has been erected in nearby Dorchester Street.

Interestingly, there are still incorrect references to the idea that the little loved Southgate development of the 1970s was a result of bomb damage and post-war clearance. It was not. Old Southgate survived almost intact after the bombing; it was the adjacent area that was burnt out and was replaced by the bus station. Bath is not the only city where anything subsequently accused of being of questionable architectural value that was built in the 1960s and '70s is sometimes excused by the fact that it had to be built because what was there before was destroyed in air raids. As has already been mentioned, the gaps in the Georgian architectural jewels such as the Royal Crescent were easily reconstructed. More damage to Bath's heritage was done by demolition in the 1960s and '70s than by bombs in the 1940s. Although old Southgate had by the 1970s seen many unsympathetic changes to the frontages of the buildings, the buildings themselves were mostly early 19th century and had not been flattened by the Blitz.

THE BOMBING OF BATH

The publication of *The Bombing of Bath* in 1983 generated some further publicity on the topic. The author received various invitations to give talks on the subject and led a walking tour as part of the Bath Festival. Perhaps the most interesting portent for the future was an invite to address the drivers of the various coach tours that did trips around Bath, on the basis that an increasing number of tourists were aware of the air raids and wanted to ask questions about them.

Time moved on. The author wrote a further book, *The Baedeker Blitz*, in 1992, on all of the Baedeker air raids – Exeter, Canterbury, York and Norwich as well as Bath. A few years later, having moved away from Bath, there was a telephone call out of the blue from the BBC to assist in the making of a programme on the Baedeker Blitz as part of the 'One foot in the Past' series. The BBC decided to focus on two specific cities. Naturally the author suggested Bath but was told that as the presenter Dan Cruickshank had already decided that one of them would be Exeter then the other must be York or the BBC might be accused of a Southern bias.

A steady diet of Blitz memories was served up by the local newspapers, notably the *Bath Chronicle*, on the annual anniversary of the air raids. The 50th anniversary in 1992 produced not only a special insert from the newspaper but also a reprint of the *Bath Chronicle* of April 27 1942. The local ITV station also broadcast a dramatised account of one survivor's memories entitled 'Harry Lambert's War'.

The same year also saw the unveiling of the first major memorial to the Blitz dead in Bath. The site of the Scala air raid shelter in Oldfield Park that had taken a direct hit in 1942 had reverted to being a simple grassed over area after the war; the Scala cinema itself became a supermarket and at the time of writing is now the Co-operative store; Scala. There was some talk over the post-war years of what to do with the site. One idea was to build a new and larger local library there. There continued to be talk that nothing should be put on the site because of the erroneous belief that bodies still lay under the soil. The decision was eventually taken to turn the site into a Memorial Garden with benches and trellis work from which wreaths are now hung. In April 1992 the then mayor of Bath, Dennis Lovelace, officially opened the Memorial Garden. A plaque commemorates the event and dedicates the area 'in memory of those who lost their lives in the raids on 25, 26, and 27 April 1942'. Thus it commemorated all, or most of, the Blitz dead rather than just those killed on that particular site.

Other stray contacts occurred. In 2000 a fine art student at Bath Spa University College, James Buddell, got in contact as he was putting on an audio visual exhibition dedicated to the victims of the Bath Blitz. The centre piece was a suspended glass bomb alongside original photographs from the time and written recollections. Many were newly collected accounts inspired by the exhibition; others included all the accounts from *The Bombing of Bath* which Mr. Buddell typed up and put on to a floppy disc which eventually ran into hundreds of pages of accounts. There was talk of applying for a grant to put all this material on to the internet and add an interactive map. There was even talk of displaying the glass bomb at the Shaftesbury Road Memorial Garden with slide and video projections against buildings.

In 2004, as another example of the spread of media, Bath Victoria Art Gallery put on an exhibition entitled 'Blitzed! War Artists in Bath' which featured the work of various artists that had produced art in relation to Bath and the raids, notably John Piper.

The rise of the internet has revolutionised the way not only in which history can be stored but possibly more importantly the way it can be shared. Memories of the Blitz can now be accessed by anyone with an internet connection. The massive BBC 'People's War' is but one, if a very impressive one, site that has any number of accounts of experiences of the Bath air raids.

The number of personal accounts about the bombing of Bath has mushroomed since the original publication of this book. Each one is fascinating in its own way and testament to the sheer resilience of individuals in extraordinary circumstances. They add to the existing narrative of these air raids.

When *The Bombing of Bath* was first published, it made use in particular of local archives, national records held in the Public Record Office (now the National Archives) and the accounts of Mass Observation held by the University of Sussex based at Brighton. As in other cities, and with similar sources, a picture emerged of Bath as a city that did not expect such heavy raids, a city where perhaps everything did not work quite as smoothly during and after the raids as was claimed in the heavily censored media but a city, nevertheless, where people did cope and services did recover without any catastrophic collapse in morale. In the years subsequent to publication no massive new collection of original material has materialised to force a revisionist rethink and the above conclusions remain largely intact.

However, others have done research into aspects of the raids to add further and better detail. A number of MA studies at Bath Spa University College have looked in to the shortcomings within local government at the time of the air raids, notably in the Fire Guards system.

Special mention must be made of the work done by the historian John Penny. His thesis on the German bombing side of the attacks in particular and the RAF counter measures was based on a close study of not only British but also German Air Force records and has added greatly to our knowledge of the military aspects of the air raids. Much of his research material has been made freely available for all to access, notably on the websites of the Fishponds Local History Society and the Bath Blitz Memorial Project.

By far the most effective and far reaching initiative has been the Bath Blitz Memorial Project. Founded in 2001 it came about as an idea from a mature student at Bath Spa University, Francis Joy, who whilst doing research into the topic discovered that there was no memorial to the civilians who had died during the air raids on Bath. He wrote to the local newspaper commenting on this fact and within a short time a number of like minded people had got in touch with him. These included Brian Vowles (a retired school teacher), Doreen Williams (the daughter of the only Bath firefighter killed by the bombs whilst on duty), Ruth Haskins and Joy Stockley. By the time a group started to meet there were over 20 or so actively involved. One who came in soon after was Jim Warren who put together a website from which much of the following information is drawn.

In the first few years of the project there were numerous meetings and much successful activity with the focus on erecting a memorial and establishing a museum. A temporary exhibition in the Bath at Work Museum in April 2002 (and later displayed elsewhere in the city), war walks through various parts of the city, a limited edition of a video of wartime memories which featured Ruth Haskins and another video 'Bath at War' produced as a joint venture between the project and 1st Take (*www.1st-take.com*) all helped to drum up both interest and money for the project. There was also a fund raising concert at the Rondo theatre organised by Doreen Williams.

The project actively explored the idea of getting the council to turn the former labour exchange on the corner of James Street West and Milk Street into a museum. This would have been most appropriate as the building had been severely damaged during the raids and still bore the shrapnel scars. When this proved impossible the project successfully applied to English Heritage for the labour exchange to be listed as being unique in Bath as a wartime building that had been neither restored nor demolished. This they were successful in doing and the building is now Grade II listed thus preventing it from being casually demolished. The idea of a Museum of Bath is in abeyance however. The project still retain some 30 or so display boards along with actual items from wartime Bath including helmets, first aid packs, a stirrup-pump and even a money box with the coins melted inside from the heat of the fires. It is envisaged that these could form a display within a Museum of Bath that would cover all of the city's history and show there was more to Bath than just the Romans and the Georgians; but a museum would cost a lot of money and would be a decision for Bath Council.

The plan for a memorial was successful although not without some problems along the way. The first thought had been to mount a memorial towards the centre of the city and at a location which had some significance to the Blitz. An obvious site was a small piece of land next to the Abbey Church House in Westgate Buildings, a building which had itself suffered severe damage during the raids with its frontage sliced off by a bomb. After the war this had been completely restored with the land next door left derelict.

The vacant piece of land adjacent was in the shape of a truncated triangle formed by Westgate Buildings to the front and Abbey Church House and another building (then in use as a newsagent) to the other side. Too small to be used for any building site, it seemed eminently suitable; it looked out over Kingsmead, one of the worst bombed parts of Bath, and the aforementioned labour exchange was only a short distance away. A local sculptor Laurence Tindall volunteered to draw up a design free of charge that would feature the carving of a woman and children alongside a Air Raid Warden standing in a doorway and anxiously scanning the skies above. The doorway itself would mirror that of the labour exchange. To either side of the doorway the walls would hold bronze plaques with the names of the civilians who had died in the raids.

Unfortunately this memorial was not to be. The project applied for planning permission for the memorial but this was refused for a number of reasons. Bath Council requested that as the city was Roman in origin and as Roman artefacts had been found nearby then there would have to be full scale archaeological excavation of the site prior to the memorial being built and that the Bath Blitz Memorial Project would have to fund this dig. In vain did the project protest that there could not be any Roman remains on the site; it was exactly where the bomb had fallen on 25 April 1942 that had demolished the front of the Abbey Church House and no ancient artefacts had been found in the consequent crater nor any found when the Church House foundations had had to be restored when it was rebuilt. The project felt that they could not afford both the cost of the memorial and the cost of a dig and an announcement to this effect was made by Francis Joy in a letter to the *Bath Chronicle* on 22 December 2002. Mr. Joy also suggested that 'the idea and suggestions from within the council that our proposed memorial was 'anti-German' is ridiculous'.

Luckily this was not the end of it. The idea was amended to focus on the memorial plaques – the lists of Civilian War Dead – rather than a full memorial and an alternate location was suggested. This was the site of the existing memorial to the military dead of both World Wars that stood at the Royal Avenue entrance to Victoria Park. There were two columns, one to either side of the existing memorial that would be suitable. The local branch of the British Legion presented no objections. Once the way was clear to erect the memorial, Francis Joy stepped down as project leader to concentrate on his studies and his role was taken over by Brian Vowles. The number of names would fit in the allocated space on the left hand column. So a design was put together by Jim Warren who ensured that the style, colour and font on the memorial were all the same as the World War Two military list of names. Its manufacture was then arranged by Mike Stockley. The names were inscribed in bronze and a suitable inscription was decided upon:

> *In memory of Bath's residents and visitors who lost their lives as a result of Air Raids on the city 1941-42.*

This was seen as appropriate. In the words of the project meeting beforehand on 14 December 2002:

> The text should encompass both residents and visitors to the city with a catch-all covering anybody omitted and should refer to 'air raids' without further detail of who conducted the raids or why.

A dedication ceremony was held on 27 April 2003. The actual unveiling of the memorial was done by the Mayor of Bath, Loraine Morgan-Brinkhurst, in a ceremony described by the *Bath Chronicle* as 'deliberately low key' with only members of the project and relatives of the victims being invited. One of the project members, Mike Stockley, told the paper that the commemoration of the Civilian War Dead in the form of the memorial plaques brought a sense of finality to 'the whole issue'. A ceremony has been held on the Sunday nearest to the date of the actual raids every year since and includes a short speech by a person who remembers the raids and the laying of flowers by a young person linked to a family that lost lives in the raid.

With money that was left over after paying for the memorial plaques, the project was able to put together two Educational Resource packs, one for secondary schools and one for primary schools, that were sent out to every appropriate school in Bath free of charge.

The website for the Bath Blitz Memorial Project, *www.bathblitz.org*, run and updated by Jim Warren, is a model of its kind. Among its strengths are a fully comprehensive section on where every high-explosive bomb fell in Bath; and an in-depth study of the not infrequent inaccuracies in the written bomb census. As the original descriptions were telephoned by and to people who were rarely locals then mistakes could occur; from simple transcriptions of 'St. Edward's Road' (when it was King Edward Road) to what appear to be complete mishearings: 'Curzon Gardens' were in fact Crescent Gardens. This echoed findings by the present author. The surveys and reports done by members of Mass Observation who visited Bath for a few days only and then reported back to London included many typographic errors of which 'Milton Street' for Milsom Street was but one; and many a talk on the bombing of Bath ended with a member of the audience looking at the copy of the map held by Bath Record Office and being understandably aggrieved that the bomb that demolished their particular house was not even correctly marked on the map.

A further invaluable resource on the site is a list of all the civilians who were killed in the Bath raids and which form the basis for the memorial plaques. Once again original lists were not always complete, nor were they always accurate. Some four months were spent by members of the project in checking every name on the list from local records as diverse as electoral registers, coroner's reports and Post Office street directories. The result was as definitive as a list as is possible. It confirmed that 417 civilians died in the bombing of Bath of which 403 can be named. It also identified two people who should have appeared on the military memorial but did not. These were Special Constable William Barrow and Edward Hall of the Royal Navy. It still threw up some ongoing research. At the time of the casting and unveiling of the memorial in April 2003 402 had been named; subsequently an extra name was identified, Leonard Oatley, a ARP warden who had lived in Tennyson Street.

The website is also a treasure trove of further eyewitness accounts of the air raids. Some have reached Mr. Warren in a variety of ways: for instance a woman who stopped him in the street who found after her father died a locked desk which was full of papers concerning his correspondence with Bath Council to ensure the street where he lived, King Edward Road, was rebuilt properly.

The main work of the project has now been done with the Memorial established, but the website continues to be updated.

The most recent initiative connected with the air raids on Bath is one that has been mirrored in other cities and that is the idea of contact with those on the German side. However, rather than a nebulous acceptance that the German air crews were simply doing their duty that had appeared elsewhere in Britain, the case in Bath has taken a rather personal slant.

Chris Kilminster had lost a number of relatives killed in the bomb that fell on the Roseberry Road shelter during the air raids. Amongst the survivors, his own mother had lost a leg and a sister, aged only four at the time, had recounted the tale of being blown out of the shelter and then seeing people she had assumed were asleep at the side of the road. These of course had been dead bodies.

As a result, Mr. Kilminster became very interested in the whole topic of the Bath air raids and has done much research into them. For many years he also would hold a service of Remembrance at Roseberry Road. In recent years this service moved to the Shaftesbury Road Memorial Park – the site of the Scala air raid shelter – and in preparation for the service on the anniversary of the raids in April 2008 he put all the details on the internet.

These details were read in Germany and by a series of contacts the upshot was that eventually Mr. Kilminster found himself talking on the telephone, via an interpreter, to a retired German Air Force pilot, Willi Schludecker, who had taken part in both of the raids on Bath on 25 April 1942 and now wanted to visit the city to apologise for his actions.

He had already performed a similar act in York in April 2007 as a form of contrition for bombing that Baedeker target as well; but that had not involved direct contact with a relative of some of the casualties and as Mr. Kilminster put it, this was a difficult request; after all the raids had killed members of his family. However after a week's thought he accepted Willi Schludecker's request; as Mr Kilminster put it to the *Times* concerning his relatives; 'I find it difficult to talk about. It still chokes me up. But there are no hard feelings against Willi. He was just doing his job and he was never a member of the Nazi party.'

Accordingly the former wartime pilot was invited over. Mr. Kilminster took him up to see the graves of the civilian dead at Haycombe cemetery and then he took part in the service at the Shaftesbury Road Memorial Park which was attended by over 200 people. The service attracted media attention across the world. The *Times* reported 'German bomber pilot Willi Schludecker says: I'm so sorry' and many papers quoted him as saying, 'There is no other way for me than to ask you all for forgiveness for any pain that I might have caused or any damage that I might have inflicted when I came to your city.' To commemorate this event Mr. Kilminster added a second plaque, at his own expense, to the existing one in the Memorial Park, which mentioned Willi Schludecker's attendance and in inscribing a dedication to 'all those who lost their lives during air raids over the city in 1941 and 25th – 27th April 1942' went beyond the first plaque of 1992 which had only mentioned the Baedeker victims of 1942.

That this visit was simply yet another stage in the ongoing commemoration of – and research into – the bombing of Bath can be illustrated by a further story. Willi Schludecker mentioned on a number of occasions during his visit and to various newspapers that as his unit was being briefed before taking off, they were told that Bath was being bombed in part because Winston Churchill, the Prime Minister, was supposedly staying in the Empire Hotel or elsewhere in the centre of the city. Churchill was in fact nowhere near Bath throughout this entire period which he spent in and around London but it is another good and interesting rumour to add to many others.

It can be confidently argued therefore that the concern raised in the final paragraphs of the first edition of this book that memories would fade and memorials would not come to be has not proved to be the case. The Memorial Project continues to add to its website, notably with an ongoing street by street analysis of which buildings were damaged. If the Museum of Bath ever comes to fruition the project is ready to supply its information boards and artefacts.

The air raids will never be central to Bath's history as they are say in Coventry (which actively uses the slogan 'City of peace and reconciliation'); Bath has simply got too many other competing claims to history and the Romans and Georgians do attract the tourists. However as long as accounts survive and people gather each year on the anniversary of the raids at the memorials that now exist, then the suffering and losses incurred in the bombing of Bath will not be forgotten.

Bibliography

Primary Sources

Guildhall, Bath: many documents and letters. In particular: bomb
census, damage charts, casualty lists, incident reports.
Public Record Office, London: documents on the raids. In particular:
      HO 192 8652
      HO 192 863
      HO 192 1651
Also documents on the relevant British fighter bases.
Bundesarchiv, West Germany: details of German attack force.
BBC archives, Reading: German radio broadcasts of the raids.

Newspapers:
      Bath and Wilts Chronicle and Herald
      Bath Weekly Chronicle and Herald
      Daily Express
      Daily Mail
      Daily Mirror
      The Daily Telegraph
      The Times
      Western Daily Press

Pamphlets:
Air Raid Precautions, Bath, Mendip Press, 1941
Bath and District Joint Planning Committee, *A Plan for Bath*, Bath,
    Pitman, 1945
City of Bath Girls' School Magazine, April 1943
Foulkes, C. H.: *Commonsense and the ARP*, London, HMSO, 1938
Mayor of Bath: *The Government's Evacuation Scheme*, 1939
Ministry of Information: *Ourselves in Wartime*, London, Odhams Press,
    1942
Ministry of Home Security: *The Fire Guards Handbook*, London,
    HMSO, 1942, *Shelter at Home*, London, HMSO, 1941, *After the
    Raid*, London, HMSO, 1940, *Evacuation: Why and How*, London,
    Lord Privy Seal's Office, 1939
Underdown, T. H.: *Bristol Under Blitz*, Bristol, Arrowsmith, 1942
Walker, G. (Ed): *Motor Cycling Magazine, July 1942*, London, Temple
    Press, 1942

War Damage Commission: *Damage to Lands and Buildings*, London, HMSO, 1941

Wimhurst, C.: *The Bombardment of Bath*, Mendip Press, 1942

Secondary Sources

Ashworth, C.: *Military Airfields of the South-west*, Cambridge, Patrick Stephens, 1981

Calder, A.: *The People's War: Britain 1939-45*, London, Granada Publishing, 1969

Collier, B.: *The Defence of the United Kingdom*, London, HMSO, 1948

Harrison, T.: *Living Through the Blitz*, London, Collins, 1976

Hastings, M.: *Bomber Command*, London, Michael Joseph, 1979

Hornby, W.: *Factory and Plant*, London, HMSO, 1958

Irving, D.: *The Destruction of Dresden*, London, Corgi Books, 1971

Irving, D.: *Hitler's War*, London, Hodder and Stoughton, 1977

Jones, R. V.: *Most Secret War*, Hamish Hamilton, 1978

Kohan, C. M.: *Works and Buildings*, London, HMSO, 1952

Laurie, P.: *Beneath the City Streets*, London, Granada Publishing, 1979

Lee, A.: *Blitz on Britain*, London, 4 Square, 1960

Lochner (Translator): *The Goebbels Diaries*, London, Hamish Hamilton, 1948

MacInnes, C. M.: *Bristol at War*, London, Museum Press, 1962

Maclaine, I.: *Ministry of Morale*, London, George Allen and Unwin, 1979

Mosley, L.: *Backs to the Wall*, London, Weidenfield and Nicholson, 1971

O'Brien, T.: *Civil Defence*, London, HMSO, 1955

Painter-Downes, M.: *London War Notes* 1939-45, London, Longman, 1971

Pile, General Sir F.: *Ack-ack*, London, Harrap, 1949

Price, A.: *Luftwaffe*, London, Macdonald and Co., 1969

Rawnsley, C. F. and Wright, R.: *Night Fighter*, London, HMSO, 1953

Richards and Saunders: *R.A.F. 1939-1945*, Vol. I, London, HMSO, 1953

Smith, D.: *Military Airfields of Wales and the North-west*, Cambridge, Patrick Stephens, 1981

Webster and Frankland: *The Strategic Air Offensive Against Germany, 1939-1945*, London, HMSO, 1961

Wheeler-Bennett, J.: *King George VI. His Life and Reign*, London, Macmillan, 1958

Index

AA defences *see Anti-aircraft defences*
Abbey *see Bath Abbey*
Abercrombie Report (1946) 154
Aberdeen 21
Admiralty 105,153
  buildings in Bath 10
  evacuees in Bath 2-4,63
  rents paid by 9-11
  Admiralty Home Guard 138
Africa, North 16
AI *see radar*
Airborne Interception (AI) *see radar*
Air Ministry 16
Air raids, British 17
  on Essen 17
  on Kiel 17
  on Lubeck 17,18,22,149,150,152
  on Paris 17
  on Rostock 21,22,61,98
Air raids, German:
  on Aberdeen 21
  on Bath *see Bath (bombing of)*
  on Bridport 81
  on Bristol 4,12,23,32,35
  British contingency plans against 2
  on Canterbury 112
  on Coventry 97,151,153
  on Crediton 81
  on Exeter 19,22,27,113,137,148,158
  on London (WW1) 1
  on London (WW2) 1-2,12-13,38,50
  on north-east Scotland 21
  on Norwich 112,148,158
  on York 148
Air raid shelters:
  Anderson 6,34,118
  Morrison 6,41,51,65,66,76,77,78,94,101
  mines as 2-3
  public 6,10,34,37,43,61,86,93,104 (*see also individual shelter locations within Bath*)
  quarries as 2-3
  railway tunnel as 75,109

Air Staff, German 18 *see also German High Command*
Alexandra Park 96
Alstadt (Lübeck) 18
Ambulance service (in Bath) 8,10,53-54,59,63,64,73,77-78,84,130
Anderson shelters *see air-raid shelters*
Angel, Mr. 45
Angus, Wally 39,44,55,72,73
Anti-aircraft (AA)defences 4-5,11,23-24,81
  at Bristol 21-24,28,81
  at Cardiff 28,81
  at Portland 22,26,79
  at Portsmouth 28
Apsley House 6,7,36,59,60,63,84,145
Assembly Rooms 1,74,91,135,
  closed at War's out-set 9
  bombing of 93
  conflagration 99,103,150,154
Astley-Weston, Dr. Bernard 36,60,122,136
Avon, River 23,25
Avon Street 114

'Baedeker' raids 1,98,149,150,158,166 *see also Air raids (German)*
Baker, Freda 124
Barrow, Mr. (special constable) 48
Barton Motors 65
Bateman, Aubrey (Mayor of Bath) 135
Bath *passim, et:*
  anti aircraft defences 114
  defences 12-14,18,114
  evacuations from 116-117
  evacuees in 10-13,16-18,67, 137-138,146
  North 63
  Roman relics in 1
  wartime population 2 *see also Civil Defence organization and individual street, building and area names*
Bath, bombing *of passim, et:*
  false alarms 1,4

early bombs 4,5
reasons for 6
longer term consequences 137-154
funds donated to victims 143
British aircraft losses 24
German aircraft losses 32-35, 79-81
investigators from London 99-100,131,138
news of in London 62-63
newspaper reactions to 62,137,149
summary of damage 150-151*see also Casualties, Civil Defence organisation, Shock victims*
Bath (Maine, Inn) 143
Bath, Herbert 11,100
Bath Abbey 113,132,134,153,154,162
Abbey Church House 41,88,150,154,162,163
Abbey Churchyard 132
Bathampton 78,113
station 113
Bath City football ground 12
Bath corporation 147
Batheaston 9,99
Bathford 3,74
Bath Spa railway station 45,88,99
Bath stone 2,57,72,136,142
Bathwick School 10
Bartle of Britain 11
Bear ambulance depot 55
Bear Flat 39,93,94,104,106
Bear Garage 39
Beaufighter (aircraft) 24,26,27,79-80
Beechen Cliff 44,76,93,135,138
Beechen Cliff Place 94,95,96,154-155
Beer Head 26
Bellots Road 41,42,45,46
Blackburn, Mr. 96
Blake, Mr. and Mrs. Frank 111
Blitz, London *see London (bombing of)*
Bloomfield Road 104
Bomber Command 15-

18,21,61,149,150 *see also RAF*
Bombing of civilians
(as policy) 15,17
daytime 15
night-time 158 *see also Air raids, Bath (bombing of), Luftflotte III*
Bombs:
high-explosive 32,37,40,47,56,85,88,90-93,150,152,164
incendiary 12,17,32,35,37,38,40,45,52,54,56,61,71,77,84,85,88,90,91-92,111,152
jettisoning by Germans of 5,12,26
time 15,97
Bournemouth 128
Bradford-on-Avon 2,3,27,74
Bridges, Mrs. 79
Bridport 84
Bristol 5,139
AA guns at 23,26,28,29,32
air raids on 5,12,13,23,27
Bath casualty lists published in 138
Bath evacuees housed in 75,115
help sent to Bath from 45,77,81,85,100,122,132
see also Health (Bristol Minister of)
Bristol Temple Meads station 115,134
Bristol University 132
British Museum 3
Brook Road 41,42,58
Brougham Hayes 72
Brougham Hayes Bridge 47
Brown's Folly 3,75,81
Bruselis/Evere 21
Burden, William 4,10,72
Bus station 154

Camden Road 134
Canterbury 112,148,158
Cardiff 28,81,133
Casualties (in Bath):
first in War 21
in first raid 31,33,40,44
in second raid 45,47,48,53,55-57,59,62

in third raid 68,72,75,83,85,
92-93,99,100
overall 120-122,131,148,151
lists published in Bristol 138 *see
also Shock victims*
Catherine Place 126
Chancellor House 41
Chancellors Yard 41
Charmy Down:
airbase at 5,111
aircraft from 23,24,152
Chelsea Road 38,39
Cheltenham Street 45,50,129,148,
154
Chequers (public house) 147
Chilcompton 114
Chippenham 27
Churchill, Winston, Mr. 15,150,167
Circus, the 92,114,150,154
Citizens' Advice Bureau 132
City of Bath Boys' School 10,
105-106,117,144
City of Bath Girls' School 105,155
Civil Defence organisation (in
Bath) 5,6,11,22,23,31,36,38,44,
53,59,60,63,64,77,84,100,111,
136,137,147
Claremont Methodist Church 134
Claremont Road 107
Clayton, Jill 58,74,75,131
on dropping of first bombs 34
on experience of shock 62
on returning to Bath 103-104
on the devastation 118
Clyde Buildings 143
Coleman, Emily 36,75
Coleman, Sidney 36,38,75,93
Colerne:
airbase at 5,26,31,32,64,111
aircraft from 23,152
helpers sent from 64,131
Combe Down 63
tunnel 75
Combe Park 83
Comfortable Place 148
Cooper, Mr. and Mrs. 106,133
Corfield, the Misses 128
Coronation Avenue 69
Corsham 2

Corston Methodist Chapel 104
Courageous, HMS 9
Coventry 63,151,167
bombing of 97
Coventry Cathedral 153
Crediton 84
Crescent Gardens 35,54,62,71,164
Cutting family (of Kingsmead
Terrace) 134
Cutting, Ivor 102
Cutting, Mr. 102

Daily Telegraph 61
Dando, Mr. and Mrs. 55
Davies, Eric 57,69,82
on dropping of first bombs 31
on destruction of Gasworks 42
on bomb in Eleanor Place 50-51
on being rescued from the rubble 67
on family's injuries 71
on evacuating from Bath 110
on tracking down looters 142-3
Davies, Rhys, MP 149
Davis, Albert:
on German machine-gunning 53
on the operations of the rescue
squads 121,125
Davis, John 124
Davis, Private 124
Defiant (aircraft) 5,69-81
Delve, Florence 51,82
on tragedy next door 69-70
on experience of shock 74
on moments preceding third raid 85
on roughing it with babies 108
on evacuating from Bath 115
on the terror 155
Delve, William 93
Despatch riders 36,39,41,48,59,65,
72,121,128
Devon 22,79
Devonshire Buildings 72
Dolemeads 20,43
Dolman, Faith 43,71,76,77
on flight to Twerton Round-hill
shelter 34-35
Dorchester 27
Dornier (aircraft):
Do.17s 80

Do.217s 21
Dorset 23,27,28
Dunkerton 109
Dunkirk 15

Eastbourne Avenue 107
Eastern front 15
Eastlays 3
Eleanor Place 31,50
Electric Light Works 45
Elizabeth, Queen (wife to George
   VI) 135-136
Ellis, Sir Hugh 135
Elm Grove Terrace 58,108,114,
   129,154
Empire Hotel 4,12,106,167
Englishcombe 44,76,110
Englishcombe Lane 19
Essen 12
Evacuees: from Bath 116-117
   in Bath 2,9,10-11,137-138,146
Evening Chronicle 143,151
Exeter 9,26,29,79,152,158
   bombing of 9,22,27,113,137,
   148,158
Exeter, HMS 9
Exmoor 81

Fairfield Park 134
Field, Rosalind 75
'Fighter Night' 79
Fire bombs *see Bombs (incendiary)*
Fire services (in Bath) 17,91
   in first raid 35,41
   in wake of first raid 64,80
   in second raid 58
   in wake of second raid 68-69
   in third raid 86,89
Fire stations 46,78
First aid services (in Bath)
   *see Homestead First Aid Post, Snow
   Hill First Aid Post*
Food, Ministry of 99,117
Ford family (of New King Street)
   33,125
Ford, Mr. 125,132
Foreign Office, German 149
Foresters Arms (public house) 7,63,
   84

Foxhill 4,7,63
France, fall of 11
Francis Hotel 92,120,150
Frome 140
Fry's 118
Fullers Garage 86
Full Moon (public house) 31,95,
   122
Gale, Tom 42,45,56,65,78
Gasworks 25,37,41,42,44,46,54,
   58,62,104
Gay, Sergeant 66
GCI *see radar*
Gee (navigation aid) 16
George VI 1
German High Command 61,99,153
Gingell, Edith 74
Gittens, Mr. 32
Glasshouse 63
Gloster Regiment 93
Gloucester 27
   hospital 100
Goddard, Miss 46
Goebbels, (Paul) Joseph
   18,61,98,149
Gough, Henry 108,113,133
   on devastation of Bath 111
   on suffering attentions of a looter
   141-2
Gough, Muriel 45,53,57,76,77,92,
   101,108
   on aftermath of first raid 45
   on bomb in Kingston Road 88-89
   on being freed from rubble
   101
Graf Spee 9
Grantham, P/0 80
Great Western Railway (GWR) 114
Green Park 32,86,125,150,154
Green Park Buildings 85
Green Park Station 99
Green Tree (public house) 55,72
Ground Controlled Interception
   (GCI) *see radar*
Guildhall 107,114,128,129,130,
   132,135,140,144,148
GWR 114

Haile Selassie I 143

Hamlin, Henry 44,64,121,127
Hampshire 27
Hampton Rocks 75,110
Hanover Street 148
Harden, Elizabeth 33
Harris, Arthur (C-in-C, Bomber
  Command) 16-17
Harris, William 65
Hartley, Mr. 135
Havoc (aircraft) 80
'Haw-Haw, Lord' (William Joyce)
  152
Hawkins, Edna 124
Haycombe Cemetery 101,134,152,
  155,166
Hayward, Mr. (special constable)
  37,48,75,76
Hayward, Mrs. 72
Hayward, Sam 71,76,117,135
  on decision against flight 76
  on emergency repairs 116
Head, Harry 129
Health, Bristol Minister of 68,100
Heinkel (aircraft) 80-81
Hemingway, Ivy 71
Henrietta Park 40
  shelter 10
Hereford 27
Heskins, Mrs. 34
High Command, German see
  German High Command
High Ercall 27
High-explosive bombs see Bombs
  (high-explosive)
Hitler, Adolf 11,98,99,116,150
  and bombing of Lübeck 17
  and bombing of Paris 17
  and bombing of Rostock 61,101
  orders 'terror attacks' 18
Hoenicke, Gunther
  on Luftwaffe approach to Britain 25
  on bombing of Bath 25
Holburne of Menstrie museum 11
Holloway 36,38,72,93,95,106,108,
  122,125
Holy Trinity Church 86
Home Guard 11,51,64,66,97,100,
  103,129,138,141
  see also Admiralty Home Guard

Home Security, Ministry of 61
Homestead 63,140
Homestead first-aid post 38,39,40,
  54,55,63,82,83,140,141
Honiley 27
Hope Cove 80
Horler, Grace:
  on uncertainty over mother's fate
  107,108,133
  on travelling to fetch mother from
  Bath 133
Horsell, Marjorie 39,83,111,122, 141
  on difficulties of travel during
  second raid 54
  on scalped old lady 56
Horsell, Mr. 111
Horwood, Mr. 34
Howard, Colonel 128
Howell, Mr. 34
Howells Court 59,124
Humphries, Bernard 87,119,144
Hungerford Road 37
Hunt's the Undertakers 49
Hurford, Edward 110
Hurford, Winifred 71,110
Hurricane (aircraft) 5,24,79-80,81

Illasewicz, S/Sgt. 26
Incendiary bombs see Bombs,
  incendiary
Information, Ministry of 106
Ivins, Wing Commander 80
Ivy Grove 44,69

Jackson, Hubert 4,44
  on being trapped in Morrison
  shelter 51,52
  on rescue from Morrison shelter
  69-70
  on being taken in by colleague 76
  on devastation of his home 138-139
Jackson, Mrs. Hubert 56,138
Jackson, Mr. (policeman):
  on bombing of Dolemeads 13
  on first raid 39
  on second raid 53
Jamming, radio 22
Jean (dying child) 70
Jeschonnek, Gen. Hans 17

Johnson, Colonel and Mrs. 127-128
Joyce, William ('Lord Haw Haw')
  152
Julian Road 91,147
Junction Road 55,105
Junkers-88 (aircraft) 21,79

Keynsham 10,27,105
Kiel 17
King, Lady 103
King Edward Road 50,55,73,165-166
Kingsmead East 86
Kingsmead Flats 86,154
Kingsmead Lane 85
Kingsmead School 87,141
Kingsmead Square 33,43,85
Kingsmead Street 34,74,86,118,
  124,151,154
Kingsmead Terrace 102,126,134
Kingston Road 45,76,88,111
Kingswood Gardens 76,108
Kingswood School 108
Kohn, Dr. Frederick 45,68,100
  on treatment of second-raid
  casualties 57

Labour exchange 86,161,162
Lacock 115
Lancaster (aircraft) 16
Lanion 21
Lansdown 99,134
Lansdown Crescent 150
Lansdown Road 134
Lee, Mrs. 74
Leslie, Mr. 103
Livingstone (public house) 49
Lock, Major Geoffrey 5,31
Locksbrook Road 40
Lock's furniture works 88
London 76,137
  East End of 2,10,143
  evacuees from 1,9,11,12,124
  investigators from 100,103,108,
  131
  looters from 142-143
  news of Bath's bombing 62
Long & Sons 90
Longfellow Avenue 113
Looting 130,139-43

Lost Property Office 128
Lower Bristol Road 41,42,55,76,88,
  94,99
Lower Oldfield Park 50,105
Lower Weston 6
Lubeck, bombing of 17,18,22,149,
  150,152
Luftflotte III 15,18,21,113
Luftwaffe 2,11,12,15,17-19,21,25,
  29,62,98,148,149
  transferred to Eastern front 15
  ordered to carry out 'terror
  attacks' 18
  moved from Netherlands into
  France 18
  prepares to bomb Bath 27,31
  German radio concerning 66
  returns to 'tip and run' raids 148
  see also Air raids (German),
  Luftflotte III
Lyncombe Vale 146

Machine-gunning by German
  bombers 23-24,35,38,39,40,51,
  52-53,59,68,74,80,82-83,86,94,
  110,148,152
McNair, P/O 24
Maple Grove 55
Margaret's Buildings 126
Marks, Anne 33,42,44,52,71,74,
  118
  on dropping of first bombs 37
  on deaths of Ford family 127
  on juvenile looting 140-41
Marlborough Lane 31,32,40
Marshfield 145
Mary Magdalene Chapel 93,152
Meredith, Myrtle 71,73,77,104,
  119,
  on wreckage of King Edward
  Road area 73
  on evacuating from Bath 114
Messenger service (in Bath) 7
Middlemas, Elsie 124
Middlemas, Jean 124
Middlemas, Dr. Mary 44,124
Midland Bridge 7,55,63
Midland Railway 7,41,52
Midland Railway Goods Yard 41,62

Miller, Rose
  on bomb at West Twerton School
  84-85
  on return to wreckage of her
  home 116-117
Milsom Street 144,153
Mines (around Bath) 3
Modern Motors 41
Monkton Farleigh 3
Monmouth Street 85
Moorland Road 37,49,105
Morrison shelters *see Air-raid shelters*
Mount Road 34,69,76,145
Munich crisis 4
Murray, Lieutenant 127
Murray, Patrick 151
Muse, Kathleen 77,112,138,140
  on being trapped under rubble 94
  on being rescued from rubble 95, 97
  on aftermath of raids 110
  on relocation of family 145
Mussolini, Benito 143

National Benefit Office 118
National Fire Service (NFS) 89-90
Naval Staff, German 18
Newark Works 90
Newbridge 37
Newbridge Hill 38
New British Broadcasting Station 97
New King Street 32,33,44,52,53,
  71,118,122,125
New King Street Methodist Church
  140
Neyder, F/Lt. 26
NFS *see National Fire Service*
Northampton Street 121
North Bath 59
North Parade 6
North Sea 21
Norwich, bombing of 112,148,158
Nott, Leslie 7,39,48,56,65,138
  on last moments of Scala shelter 48
  on search for Wally Angus' body 76
  on bureaucratic heavy-handedness
  129
  on finding a pair of skeletons 147
Nott, Mary 83

Octagon, the 144
Odd Down 44,145
Odins Road 145
Old Bridge 73,146
Oldfield Park 6,31,34,44,49-50,59,
  63,71,73,76,104,105,111,132,
  135,137,158
Oliver, Kay 53
Oliver, Major 135
Orange Grove 6
O'Shea, John 47,131

Pack Horse (public house) 75
Packwood, Mr. (special constable) 49
Padfield, Mr. 47
Parade Gardens 89,113,114,135
Paragon, the 44,65,122
Paris, bombing of 17
Parsons, Mr. (company director) 46
Parsons, Mr. (special constable) 48,49
Parsons & Vezey 41
Peacock, Mr. (messenger) 55
Penny, Vic 54,85,92,123
  on finding decaying body 147
Penzance 112
Percy Boys' Club 140
Pickard, Major 36
Pile, Gen. Frederick 4
Pitmans (company) 41
Plan for Bath, A 154
Plate, River, battle of 9
'Poets Corner' 93
Poland, invasion of 9
Polden, Mr. 96,97
Police station, central 6,13,36,132
Poole, Alma 31,47
Poole, Sydney 56,131
Portland 22,26,28,79
Portsmouth 28
Potter, Mrs. 9
  on evacuation from Bath 110
Primrose Hill 51,76
Prior Park Road 53
Pritchard, Mr. 96
Public shelters *see Air-raid shelters*
  and individual shelter locations
  within Bath
Pulteney Bridge 146
Pulteney Hotel 12

Pulteney Street 11
Pump Room Hotel 11
Quarries (around Bath) 3
Queen's Messengers 64,99,117
Queen Square 53,92,150,155
Radar 6,84,152
  airborne (AI) 21,24,27,80
  ground-controlled (GCI) 24,27
Radio guidance (of bombers) 22 *see
  also X-Taub*
RAF 24
  and defence of Bath 4 *(see also
  RAF Squadrons)*
  leaflet campaigns 9,149
  role in 1941-42 22,-25 *see also Air
  raids (British), Bomber Command*
RAF Squadrons:
  87 Sqadron 5,23,24,28,79,80,
    113,152
  125 Squadron 5,23,24,26,28,79,
    80,81,152
  255 Squadron 27
  307 Squadron (Polish) 22,26,29,
    79,80,81,152
Railway Hotel 67
Randell family (of Twerton High
  Street) 12
Rattray family (of Howells Court)
  59,124
Reading 4
Regina Hotel
  74,93,102,103,114,127-129,132,
  135,141,155
Rescue services, rescue posts (in
  Bath) 18,52,53,55,69,72,83,84,
  89,94-96,127,129,151
  bogus rescue squads (looters) 142
  (see also Looting)
Rest centres 45,63,69,73,75,85,99,
  106,114,144
Rivers Street 44,147
Roseberry Road 42,58,73,78,114,
  131,154,165,166
  shelter in 44,46
Rostock 21,22,61,98
Roundhill *see Twerton Roundhill*
Royal Air Force *see RAF*
Royal Crescent 89-91,99,114,150,
  154,157

Royal United Hospital (RUH)
  59,67,68,82,83,100,131
Russell, Mr. (newsagent) 102,142
Russia, invasion of 15

Sadler's Wells ballet 87,92
St. Andrew's Church 91
St. Bartholomew's Church 50,73
St. James' cemetery 121,131
St. James' Church 14,73,95-96,
  111,133,145,155,157
St. James Parade 54,60,63,146
St. John's Church house 88
St. Mark's Church 97
St. Mark's School 9
St. Martin's Hospital
  44,68,83,99,100
St. Peter's Church 13,73,100,132
Salvation Army 45
Salvation Army hostel
  45,53,57,76,88
Scala cinema 6,61,158
Scala shelter 14,43,48-50,61,73,75,
  108,130,132,135,151,153,154,
  158,166
Scotland, air raids on 21
Second Avenue 31,47,119
Self, Fred 40,61
Self, Mr. 87
Self, Tony 71
  on the devastation 121
Selwyn, Frank 38
  on early moments of first raid 37
  on aftermath of third raid 104
Selwyn, Grace 39,40,55-56,85,140
  on second-raid casualties 60
Shakespeare Avenue 93,111
Sham Castle 32
Shand, Lady 127
Shearn, Ron 95,122,131
  on shooting of men at Mary
    Magdalene Chapel 94
  on aftermath of third raid 95
Shelters *see Air raid shelters*
Shock victims 13,48,56,58,59,69,
  86,96,108,122,128,129
Short, Fred 44,46,115,119
  on emergency repairs 115
Shrewsbury 27

Sion Hill 145
Small, William 122
Smith, Doris 11,72,131
  on sheltering in railway tunnel 75
  on dealing with the corpses 131
Smith, Dorothy 10
Smith, Robert 39,100
  on 'Is this a stunt?' lady 123
  on inadvertent looting 140
Smith, William 65,76
  on second-raid casualties 55
  on unexploded bomb 104
  on 'Is this a stunt?' lady 123
  on dealing with bodies 131-132
  on finding decaying bodies 147
Smith family (of Roseberry Road) 46
Snow Hill First Aid Post 44,123
Somerset 2,27,65,115
Somerset Place 150
Southdown 31,44,59,145
Southgate 154
Southgate Street 59,92,97
Southstoke 78,85
Spa Hotel 12,75
Squadrons, RAF see RAF squadrons
Stainer, Edwin 74,144
  on first bombs 13
Stainer, Kathleen 65,71
  on conditions at City of Bath
    Girls' School 105
  on evacuating from Bath 111
Staines 107,133
Stanley Road 43,47,63,127
  shelter in 47,131
Stonehouse 110
Stothert & Pitt 4,90,99,105,115
Stroud 27,110
Supply, Ministry of 3
Swainswick 110,145
Swansea 70
Swatton, Mr. 122
Sweetenham, Walter 4,9,10,135,
  144
  on conditions at City of Bath
    Boys' School 105
  on helping provide for the needy
    117
Swindon 28

Tangmere 28
Taylor, Joan 107,133
Taylor, Mrs. 107
Taylor, Ron 52,86
Technical College (Bath) 104
Tenby 107,133,134
Tennyson Road 93
Theatre Royal 87
Third Avenue 59
Thornbank Place 50
Topham, S/Leader 28
Torquay 79
Trowbridge 27,115
Trybulec, F/Sgt. 80
Tuddenham, Don 40,73,100on
  bombing of West Twerton School
  13
  on bombing of Apsley House 60
  on shock 115
Tutt, Betty 43,52,53,74
Twerton 12,50,137
Twerton Cemetery 42
Twerton High Street 12
Twerton Roundhill Shelter 34,35,
  43,71

Upper Bristol Road 36,54,90,104,
  105,144

Victoria Park 35,131,146,163
Victoria Road 47,111
  shelter in 48
Victoria Terrace 111
Victoria Works 90
VI flying bomb 137
von Sturm, Baron Gustav Braun
  98,149

Walcot 73
  parish church 74,93
Wales 27-28,134,135
Wall, Doreen 46,51,76
  on being rescued from rubble 68
  on extended hospitalization 146
Warne, Mrs. 109
Watts, Walter 147
Webster, James 32,35,36,40,71,154
  on tackling incendiaries 35
  on finding the dead 40

Wells Road 96,99,104
Wellsway 83
Welsh Guards 99,134
Western Daily Press 62
Western front 15
Weston 6,36,37,73,74,76,82
  Lower *see Lower Weston*
Weston, Dr. 123
West Twerton School 13,48,84,116
Westwood quarry 3
Weymouth House School 100,131,
  132
Whitehall 4
Whiteley, Mark 81,105,048
Wick, Mr. 87
Wicks, Mrs. 146
Widcombe 13,75
Widcombe Hill 13
Wight, Isle of 22,28,79
Wilcox, Mr. 44,47

Wilcox, Mrs. 47
Wilkins, Mr. 96
Wiltshire 115
Wimborne 108
Winchester Road 39
Windsor Bridge 73
Women's Voluntary Service *see*
  WVS
Woodmansey, Reverend 74,93,103,
  127
Wood Street 55
Woolmer, Mrs. 40
World War I 1
WVS 64,118,130,139,145
Wyvil, P/O 27

X-Taub 22,26

YMCA 64,99,117
York, bombing of 148